CHILDREN, CONSUMERISM, AND THE COMMON GOOD

CHILDREN, CONSUMERISM, AND THE COMMON GOOD

Mary M. Doyle Roche

LEXINGTON BOOKS
A Division of
ROWMAN & LITTLEFIELD PUBLISHERS, INC.
Lanham • Boulder • New York • Toronto • Plymouth, UK

Published by Lexington Books
A division of Rowman & Littlefield Publishers, Inc.
A wholly owned subsidary of The Rowman & Littlefield Publishing Group, Inc.
4501 Forbes Boulevard, Suite 200, Lanham, Maryland 20706
http://www.lexingtonbooks.com

Estover Road, Plymouth PL6 7PY, United Kingdom

British Library Cataloguing in Publication Information Available

Library of Congress Cataloging-in-Publication Data
Roche, Mary M. Doyle.
  Children, consumerism, and the common good / Mary M. Doyle Roche.
    p. cm.
  Includes bibliographical references and index.
  ISBN 978-0-7391-2947-0 (cloth : alk. paper) — ISBN 978-0-7391-4192-2 (electronic)
  1. Advertising and children. 2. Child labor. I. Title.
  HF5415.32.R64 2009
  306.3—dc22   2009022776

∞™ The paper used in this publication meets the minimum requirements of American
National Standard for Information Sciences—Permanence of Paper for Printed Library
Materials, ANSI/NISO Z39.48-1992.

Printed in the United States of America

Contents

Acknowledgments

A S I WAS PREPARING THIS MANUSCRIPT, there was a cascade of crises in the world markets. The grandiose promises of the market were exposed as illusory and the gross mismanagement on the part of many stewards of financial institutions came to light. Inevitably, this will impact the statistics on child poverty and rates of children among the uninsured. It has forced cuts in government spending on key social services as well as on public education. It remains to be seen whether expanding insecurity will bring about greater solidarity.

During this time, the United States also elected its first African American president, Barack Obama. We were able to catch a glimpse of the dreams of the civil rights movement as they came to fruition. The moment is ripe for renewing our promises to children to shape a world in which all people can not only dream of, but realize their potential to contribute to our common good.

I am indebted to Lisa Sowle Cahill, who directed my dissertation research at Boston College on children and Catholic social teaching and who graciously read and commented on an early draft of this manuscript.

I am grateful for the encouragement I received from my colleagues in the religious studies department at the College of the Holy Cross. The college granted me a research leave without which I could never have completed *Children, Consumerism, and the Common Good.*

My thanks to Jessica Bradfield of Lexington Books for her careful attention to the manuscript and her confidence that this book can make a valuable contribution to our conversations about the well-being of children. I am thankful also for the wisdom of my peer reviewer whose constructive comments were essential in bringing this project to completion.

Finally, I dedicate this work to my family: to my parents and sisters, who did not need a book to tell them how to be faithful to family or that they had a responsibility to vulnerable others; to my husband, Dennis, who has been my most ardent supporter through the long dark days of writing; and to our children, Emma Rose and Declan, who remind us each day that children are a blessing to family and community. A special thanks to Emma Rose for using her artistic talents to choose the book's cover.

Introduction

Children in a Peaceable Kingdom

I N MAY 2002, CHILDREN AND YOUNG PEOPLE from all over the globe came to New York to the United Nations' Special Session on Children to share their stories and to call upon the world community to meet its obligations to children, obligations that had been outlined in the *Convention on the Rights of the Child*. Young people at the Special Session came with firsthand experience of harsh and inhuman working conditions, of the havoc wrought by the AIDS epidemic, and the devastation left in the wake of violent conflict. They called for an end to certain types of child labor (and a marked improvement in working conditions), to trafficking and prostitution, and to the recruitment of child soldiers. They demanded greater access to important resources: food, clothing, shelter, health care, and education.

Clearly, these young people are innocent victims of the terrible circumstances in which they find themselves. They are not personally responsible for poverty, violence, and disease. Their vulnerability to abuse and exploitation is indeed great. Yet, these children have certainly demonstrated resilience in the face of such adversity. They have become passionate advocates for justice and their own liberation from oppression. The portrayals of children and childhood that they present are much more complex than the current political rhetoric allows. They are innocent, but not naïve. These young people have experience and wisdom beyond their years. From this standpoint, one could say that their innocence, their childhood, was "lost" to the ravages of injustice. They are not directly culpable for poverty, warfare, or sexism, but they have taken on a great deal of responsibility for the immense societal changes that need to take place to overcome them. They did not come to the Special

Session to reclaim their innocence, but rather to have their voices and experiences taken seriously, to be considered full members of the communities of which they are a part, and to be respected as powerful agents of change.

In the unofficial excerpts from the Special Session, some of the young people are quoted as saying, "It would make us happy and proud. Being able to participate would give us the sense that we are respected as citizens by the government." Another participant, Alexandre Bogdan Rosu, aged sixteen years, of Romania said, "We have to be careful not to confront adults, but to show them that we can reason with them and that we are logical. And we must start working for change locally."[1] The Children's Forum message reads in part, "We pledge an equal partnership in this fight for children's rights. And while we promise to support the actions you take on behalf of children, we also ask for your commitment and support in the actions we are taking—because the children of the world are misunderstood."[2] This spirit was echoed by UN Secretary-General Kofi Annan: "To work for a world fit for children, we must work *with* children."[3] From this perspective, children are participants, cocreators of a more just world, and something more: "witnesses to our words."[4] Children witness adult commitments and concrete actions, or failures to act. They stand ready to hold adults, and each other, accountable for promises made. Even though children may not have a vote in bodies like the United Nations or as citizens in their home countries, their presence, participation in dialogue and action, and their witness are critical to the building of a world "fit for children."

We read familiar lines from the Book of the Prophet Isaiah:

> The wolf shall dwell with the lamb,
> and the leopard shall lie down with the kid,
> and the calf and the lion and the fatling together,
> and a little child shall lead them.
>
> The cow and the bear shall feed;
> their young shall lie down together
> and the lion shall eat straw like the ox.
>
> The suckling child shall play over the hole of the asp,
> and the weaned child shall put his hand on the adder's den.
> They shall not hurt or destroy in all my holy mountain;
> for the earth shall be full of the knowledge of the Lord
> as the waters cover the sea. (Isaiah 11:6–9)

"A little child will lead them." Christian communities have long reflected on these passages from the prophet Isaiah, and many are familiar with the renditions of the prophecy by the Quaker painter Edward Hicks (1780–1849). The image of a child leading the people of Israel to the fullness of God's *shalom* comes to the fore. It is a startling reversal of expectations about qualities of leadership and divine reign. The figure in these passages is not strong physically or militarily, nor is he authoritative or even wise. Influenced by contemporary cultural presumptions about children and childhood, twenty-first-century Christians are apt to focus on the presumed purity and innocence of childhood as central to the community's interpretation of these passages. This focus resonates with other Christian claims found in the gospels about the blessings awaiting the meek and humble and with Jesus's interactions with children during his public ministry. Jesus welcomes children as rightful heirs to God's kingdom.[5] This resonance of Isaiah for Christians is heightened during the Advent and Christmas seasons as the churches are steeped in the annunciation and infancy narratives of the Incarnation. The birth of a vulnerable infant in impoverished surroundings signals the in-breaking of the kingdom, confounding those in power.

Children may lead us to the peaceable kingdom, but there is more to Isaiah's vision of the messianic reign and its use of the image of the child. In the fullness of God's *shalom*, beasts that have been natural enemies will no longer be at war. Indeed, they feed together in what for Christians may serve as a powerful symbol of communion. That which threatens the child, like the asp or the adder, has lost its venom and its den becomes a play place. If Christians today are to heed the prophetic call, then the world must be a safe place for the vulnerable, of which children are emblematic. Institutions that have the potential to undermine the well-being of children must be tamed and ordered in such a way that they serve human flourishing.

The specific contexts under consideration here are the institutions of global market capitalism and the spirit of consumerism that they fuel, a context which often amplifies and exploits the vulnerability of children. Though they provide one mechanism for distributing goods and services in the community, markets, like lions and wolves, have fangs, claws, and the instinct to use them. Though market influence may have encroached on areas beyond its competence, and there is a need to curb that influence, it is unlikely that society can or should rid itself of markets altogether. So the task before us is to tame markets in such a way that they serve the well-being of human persons and communities, with special attention given to how they impact the lives of the most vulnerable among us.

Recognizing the potential insights to be gleaned from Isaiah with respect to an environmental ethic and our radical interdependence with creation, use of these passages for the current project will take a primarily anthropocentric turn: economic markets serve human persons and communities, not the other way around.⁶ The measure of ethical economic behavior is the promotion of human dignity and ultimately the common good of all creation. Children's basic well-being and their access to important services such as health care and education should not be left to the whims of Wall Street; human flourishing cannot be bought and sold on an exchange in order to maximize the wealth of a relative few. As we will see in debates about child labor, contexts in which children work to support their families should not entail risks to life and health, nor should children sacrifice education or recreation that is crucial for development. Children of privilege are increasingly the subjects and the intended audience for a billion dollar advertising industry that has profit and not well-being as its controlling value.

Children's participation in the economic life of their families and communities is a fact; can it be transformed from a threat to well-being into a benefit? This is the crux of the matter. Taking children's intrinsic human dignity seriously demands that we consider them as full, interdependent members of our communities; their participation in social life, including its economic aspects, is constitutive of justice for children and should be shaped according to their age and ability as well as the common good.

The task before us then, articulating an ethic of the common good for children in the context of consumer culture, requires that we first set the stage for these three interlocking themes: childhood, the common good, and consumer culture. First, childhood in this text is used fluidly to mean very young children and children through the period we often call adolescence.⁷ That is not to say that infants do not possess the intrinsic dignity that we claim for all children, but the focus will be on children whose age and ability allows them to participate more actively in community life. Nor does it imply that all people that fall within this age range require the same kinds of protections or can participate in the same way. As many scholars have argued, childhood is in part a social construction, a set of ideas held by adults that can shift and change across time and culture.⁸ While it is true that ideas about what constitutes childhood itself and what constitutes a good childhood may vary, it is also true that human beings in all times and places enter this phase of vulnerability and dependency that is part of our nature; we are unable to walk, talk, or care for ourselves for a significant period in our youth. Injustice occurs when natural vulnerabilities are exploited and become social vulnerabilities that lead to marginalization or exclusion. For example, children's small stature should not be taken advantage of by mining companies or carpet factories. Children's inability to assert themselves in legislative debate ought not mean they are without articulate and vigorous representation.

If children are to be free to be leaders in their communities, calling us to peace and reconciliation, as Isaiah's prophecy claims and as the children in attendance at the UN Special Session attest, then we will need a vision of what childhood is and can be that avoids both an idealized vision of children's innocence that diminishes their moral and spiritual agency and those images that overestimate children's savvy and resilience (both of which shape how we think about children's economic participation in the community). The first romantic image may lead us to isolate and marginalize some children in ways that fail to enhance their flourishing, often in the name of protection. The latter view allows us to abdicate our responsibilities toward some children and exact harsh disciplinary measures that consign them to vicious cycles of poverty and exclusion.

Media attention around children, when it does not cover them as victims of the violence or carelessness of others, investigates them as perpetrators. That we are as horrified by youth crime and violence, some of which has been especially gruesome, suggests that the fact of such violence remains an anomaly, an exception to the rule. However, our insistence in defining children by their innocence has caused a faltering response to the needs of some vulnerable children in our communities. Members of youth gangs, for example, do not fit our image of childhood. If children are by their nature innocent and so unaccountable for many of their actions, then these children must be categorized by society as something other than children. The troubling trend in the United States is the trial and incarceration of these young people as adults.[9] Another challenge to the world community is formulating an appropriate response to the phenomenon of child soldiering in which young people are involved in unimaginable crimes against humanity. Their rehabilitation is an arduous process but a necessary one if these young people are to be brought together with their families and communities in a safe way. While it remains more often the case that children are the victims of the sinfulness and violence of others, in both of these cases, children are said to have "lost" their childhood and it is not easily reclaimed.[10] What often goes unexamined is what kind of childhood we imagine is good for children and how securing such a childhood experience might be achieved in varying cultural and socioeconomic contexts.

Historian Viviana Zelizer, in her frequently cited *Pricing the Priceless Child*, brings together shifting views of childhood and places these in an economic context. As the emphasis on the vulnerability of children grew, so did their emotional value for families and communities. Looking to children for economic value detracted from the romantic ideal and could be interpreted as a sign of parental indifference. Children's role in the family was to provide emotional gratification for parents and other family members who could delight in their simplicity and the escape they provided from the stressful world of business (though this relief was primarily for fathers who faced the stress of work outside the home as opposed to the stresses and strains of child rearing as arduous work done on the part of mothers and other domestic servants).

Scholars researching ancient and medieval sources have stressed that during these periods in history there is evidence that parents loved their children and developed strong emotional attachments to them. That children worked and contributed to the family's financial well-being should not necessarily be taken as a sign of parental disregard.[11] In the family economy, children had long functioned as heirs to family land and property, as laborers on farms and with livestock, and also as producers of goods in household industries. Children earned their keep. With industrialization this question of children's ability to participate in the economy became much more problematic as the tendency to exploit children became increasingly obvious. Perhaps this is because exploitation in the family and home is more easily hidden from view than is factory work. Children's factory work as "wage labor" benefited not only their families but also, and perhaps primarily, the companies that employed them.

The image of the factory child or the chimney sweep, so far from the romantic ideal of a child lavishing in the glory of creation, would stir philanthropists and governments to action on behalf of children, though their motives for "saving" children were quite often mixed. In any case, the romantic ideal we have inherited has contributed to an outcry against exploitative child labor. A child's innocence and emotional value for parents and families now preclude them from having any economic value in terms of contributions from their labor. Though there is a worldwide movement to abolish exploitative child labor, the tension between children's economic and emotional value persists, revealing more ambivalence than many of us would like to admit.

In the U.S. context as elsewhere, there remained several exceptions to the exclusion of child labor. Many children, especially young girls, worked in the home as caretakers of younger children and in "cottage" industries. As with their mothers, it would be some time before this work was ever really recognized as such, and even now it remains unclear at what point such labor in the home becomes exploitative. Farming interests also pressured to have labor done on the family farm excluded from any legislation. This was certainly influenced once again by the powerful image from romanticism that idealized children living in the country and pastoral settings. That farming could be dangerous for children is overshadowed by this romantic image. Child actors are another example of children who work with social approval.[12]

A romantic image of the child had firmly taken hold by the late nineteenth and early twentieth centuries, leading to what Viviana Zelizer calls the "sacralization" of children.[13] Child labor was a violation of the sacred child. As children's economic value for their families went on the decline, their emotional value increased. Children went quickly from being economically "worthless," that is being a pure financial drain on their parents, to being emotionally "priceless."[14] Though the care of children was and is certainly expensive, the emotional satisfaction that one receives from children is worth the price. Combined with compulsory education laws, the image of the innocent child allowed even lower-class children to live in the "non-productive world of childhood."[15] Zelizer notes that "the proper place for a 'sacred' child was a protected environment, segregated from adult activities," like the school and the playground.[16]

The tension between children's economic and emotional worth persists in the current debate about the well-being of children and is as complex as ever, as we will see in the coming chapters. Movements addressing child labor have witnessed dramatic shifts in perspective, reclaiming the economic contributions of children as having legitimate personal and social value. In communities of privilege, children are reared in the habits of consumerism. In the United States this often means buying materials for children here that are made by children elsewhere. Children's participation in the economy, by desiring certain products, is thought of as critical for the success of the market. Their emotional worth for adults has also no doubt contributed to outrageous spending on the part of many parents and to the burgeoning fertility industry.[17] The emotional and economic values of children are not mutually exclusive, but are rather in constant interrelation. Attention to their interaction prompts new and important questions about children's involvement in economic life.

Acknowledging this history and the tensions between our operating images of childhood is crucial if we are to navigate an adequate ethic for children and the common good in the context of market capitalism. We must be alert to the ways in which we imagine what is good for children can often be influenced by conceptions of gender, race, and class. The manipulation of images allows the community to distance itself from some children (members of gangs and child soldiers, for example) and deny any accountability for their behavior or responsibility for securing their well-being. Long-time advocate of children and critic of U.S. education policy Jonathan Kozol has put the point most forcefully:

> Some writers even raise a question as to whether children here [in poor, minority communities of New York City] may constitute a group so different from most other children, with a set of problems (or, we are told, "pathologies") so complicated, so alarming, so profound, that they aren't "children" in the sense in which most of us use that word, but that they're really "premature adults," perhaps precocious criminals, "predators," we are told by those who are supposed to know. It strikes me as a dangerous exaggeration that may seem to

justify a differentiation in the pedagogies and the social policies that are enacted or applied within such neighborhoods, with greater emphasis on rigid discipline than on the informality and intellectual expansiveness that are familiar in the better schools that educate the children of rich people.[18]

Within theological disciplines, these paradoxes in how we think about the nature of children and childhood have been closely critiqued in a dialogue that has emerged within the field of practical theology. Practical theology begins with concrete moral questions and experiences, and brings them to "classic" sources and then turns forward to "strategic practical theological reflection about ways to proceed with concrete and faithful action in the future."[19] The goal is transformation at both personal and social levels. Bonnie J. Miller-McLemore notes,

> A practical theology of children has the role of mediating between powerful religious symbol systems and the wider society. It tries to bridge the gap that sometimes arises between the efforts of systematic theologians to shape a Christian worldview and the daily practices that actually form such a world. . . . The aim is to understand what is going on in order to effect change in a situation and in the theological ideas that define it.[20]

The method of practical theology makes it a particularly fruitful dialogue partner for ethical reflection emerging from the traditions of Catholic social teaching which follows a similar hermeneutical circle that begins with experience. The value placed on experience as a source of moral reflection also provides some common ground with feminist theology and other theologies of liberation that often shape the turn to Catholic social teaching.

Practical theologians have brought the theological insights of traditions within Christianity to bear on questions regarding children's place in our families and congregations as well as the nature of our obligations toward children in our families and communities; as well as the children of strangers and enemies. Miller-McLemore in particular has faced squarely the question of children's participation in human sinfulness, taking their moral agency seriously, thereby paving the way for children to fully participate in practices of reconciliation and justice. She notes that we are charged with "raising imperfect children in an imperfect world."[21] Drawing on her own experience as a mother and theologian, she has perceptively deconstructed images of childhood innocence and depravity found in the Christian traditions on childhood, prompting religious communities to reflect on the moral and spiritual dimensions of child rearing.[22] Don Browning and his collaborators in the Lilly Project on Religion, Culture, and the Family at the University of Chicago have analyzed trends in marriage and family law, sociological research, and insights from evolutionary biology to discern their impact on parenting strategies and the well-being of children. Marcia Bunge gathered scholars from across the theological disciplines, from within Protestant and Catholic Christianity, to mine the traditions for resources with which to enrich our thought about children and our moral obligations toward them.[23] Pamela Couture has been particularly articulate in defending children's rights, placing these within a theological framework that values individual dignity and key social relationships. She addresses the need to combat child poverty through institutions that include but move beyond the family and congregation.[24] Finally, John Wall proposes thinking about our ethical obligations to children from within a covenantal perspective.[25]

Building on the insights from this ongoing conversation, the theological anthropology of childhood that will be developed here can be summarized in the following. As human beings whose dignity is real in the present, not purely nascent potential, children are created good by God and are vulnerable to sin that is both personal and social. Their dependence on others is a mark of their humanity, not only of their youth. Their dignity arises in the context of this vulnerability and not in spite of it.[26] *Inter*dependence is rarely valued in a culture that prizes independence, autonomy, self-reliance, and control. Having to depend on others to accomplish the tasks of daily living is regarded as a loss of one's dignity. Such dependence is often brought to relief in the very young, the very old, and the disabled. It is a task of the Christian community to see how human dignity shines through vulnerability and demand that such dignity be recognized in concrete communal practices. This moves us toward a more adequate theological anthropology—a vision of the human person fully alive and flourishing in community—that can account for and celebrate the dignity of children as full participants in the common good of society.

Flowing from the commitment to intrinsic human dignity and the radically social nature of human personhood is the second of our interlocking themes, the tradition of the common good which shapes how persons live together in society. This will receive more substantial treatment in chapter 3, but we can set out some broad definitions and distinctions here. In the economic context, the common good in the Catholic moral tradition demands more nuance than the utilitarian theories that govern market rationale. The common good envelops the social conditions that promote the flourishing of all people in their communities. The common good is not simply the greatest good for the greatest number. Such a utilitarian calculus can tolerate deep sacrifice on the part of some to maximize pleasure for the many, who in reality may not be the "many" at all but rather the few who are in positions of power and privilege. Meanwhile, the same groups of people are asked to bear the burden of sacrifice time and time again. Children are often in this category along with women, people of color, and the poor.[27]

While striving for the common good certainly entails sacrifice, the burdens of such sacrifice should be shared and cannot be born to the point where one's basic human dignity is undermined. As the sacrifice is shared, so are the fruits of common life. These goods are distributed according to the norms of justice. While a market economy may distribute more to some than to others, no person or community may fall below the threshold of goods required for a dignified life. Because the common good tradition responds to the embodied, relational, and transcendent aspects of human personhood, and because it seeks the conditions that allow for flourishing (or what Vatican II called "perfection"), achieving the common good will demand more than bare subsistence living.

The requirements of the common good go beyond the just distribution of the community's resources. Not only are all members of the community to receive goods for well-being, all members are called to contribute to the building up of those goods according to their unique ability. Participation and interdependence are themselves human goods. Children are full members of their communities (family, neighborhood, school, marketplace, house of worship, etc.). As vulnerable members, children—especially poor children—have the most urgent claim on our resources. This is not a particularly contested claim even though children often compete with other groups, like the elderly, for goods and services. The claim that children should also be full participants in our families and communities is more complex especially when we consider the marketplace. Nevertheless, in the common good tradition, participation is a constitutive element of justice and so communities must strive to encourage the participation of children and young people in our common life in ways that serve their flourishing. At a minimum, children's experiences, voices, needs, and desires should be included in our conversation about how best to live and share together.

The introduction of the common good tradition to the dialogue is significant for a number of reasons. The concept has been developed among secular theorists as well as religious ethicists. As Catholic ethicist David Hollenbach has demonstrated, the language of the common good can bridge the cultural and religious differences that often stymie ethical debate, allowing parties to reach agreement on concrete issues that impact human flourishing.[28] This typifies the natural law confidence in human reason and ability to discern the good for persons and communities that may be more prevalent in Catholicism than in Protestant denominations where there tends to be more skepticism about fallen human nature. As developed within Catholic social teaching, the common good also provides language to address the need for institutional transformation that includes, but is not limited to personal conversion. So, thinking about issues facing children in both local and global contexts can benefit from insights in this tradition. At the same time, the tradition itself might stand to benefit from bringing the concerns of childhood to the center of the wider common good discussion.

Finally a word about the consumer culture that is largely shaping many areas of our common life and increasingly provides the dominant context for children's social participation. Ethicist Kenneth Himes has recently reviewed literature on this phenomenon and he highlights several features that merit mention at the outset of our analysis. Consumerism can be considered a social movement, an ideology, or a way of life. The analysis here will focus primarily on the latter two modes of thinking about consumerism. As an ideology, consumerism is "a way for talking about a market mentality that defends individuals' freedom of choice and entrepreneurship while criticizing economic models like communism, socialism, or other approaches that interfere with rational agents making decisions in minimally regulated free markets."[29] This particular view of participation in markets is bolstered using rights rhetoric, which is then manipulated in such a way that it exploits children as we will see in the context of advertising to children. Children have the "right" to advertising and to various products. The task of the community is primarily to train young people in the exercise of their many choices. As a way of life, consumerism focuses on the "benefits and pleasures of material affluence" that now borders on a "pathological preoccupation."[30] This is the "more is better" theory in which material wealth, possessions, and the ability to hire out various tasks (think here of cooks, cleaners, gardeners, personal trainers, child care, etc.) is a mark of status and forms the basis of other social relationships. The result is that many of our daily interactions are conducted contractually, in market terms. Various terms have been coined to describe this way of life: conspicuous consumption, competitive consumption, or affluenza.[31]

Consumer culture extends the language of the market into spheres of life once considered immune from its influence, namely the home and hearth. These had provided refuge for men who faced the harsh world of business. Wives and mothers were to provide a humanizing influence and a logic of love at home. When consumerism becomes a way of life, anything (or anyone) can become an object of exchange in the market and "consumer" replaces "citizen" as a central feature of political self-understanding, and may be replacing other identities such as "student" or "disciple" as well.[32] With regard to the impact of consumer culture on children and notions of childhood, Juliet Schor takes this claim one step further, noting that according to Marxist economic theory a commodity is not merely an object of exchange, but is also an object "produced specifically for the purpose of exchange."

According to Schor, "the cultural category of childhood itself is produced for the purpose of being sold." Advertising professionals are "creating, transforming, and packaging childhood as a productive cultural concept that they then sell to the companies that make the actual products that children buy."[33]

As we have already noted, human beings require a number of goods for our basic well-being and indeed our flourishing. We must consume to survive and thrive. The phenomena that we are describing here is a distortion of right relationships with each other and with the world around us. Consumption among the privileged is often grossly out of proportion to our needs, comes at the expense of others, and threatens the very sustainability of the environment. When we investigate children as consumers and children as laborers in chapter 1, we see a dark underside of consumption: poor children are themselves consumed. These forms of overconsumption become what Himes refers to as the "ugly twin of poverty," literally seen today in the rise of childhood obesity and diabetes to epidemic proportions in the United States.

Our Way of Proceeding

The language of the common good, with its emphasis on interdependence, rights, and responsibilities has the needed nuance to address the needs of real children at both local and international levels. It is able to engage competing claims about the nature of childhood that are obscured in both liberal human rights and family values rhetoric. To discern the common good for children today, this project takes up the method of Catholic social teaching, the hermeneutical circle or the "see, judge, act" model of moral decision making, which as we have seen follows the trajectory of the conversation on childhood within the field of practical theology.

We begin by trying to "get the story right." This demands that we begin with the experiences of children. For many of us this means spending time listening to the children in our lives. It also demands that we spend time with those (if not ourselves) who have ventured to hear the stories of children we may never personally know, who live in conditions of poverty, illness, and violence that are barely imaginable. To put these narratives in perspective we look to the big picture revealed in data provided by agencies who advocate for children. Next, we interpret these stories in light of the gospel and a commitment to the common good. Through this process of discernment we gain a clearer picture of the kinds of policies and programs that can advance the well-being of children. We engage these practices, evaluate them, and the cycle begins anew, hopefully spiraling deeper toward the root causes of children's exploitation, and farther toward the realization of God's peaceable kingdom.

Chapter 1 explores what the Second Vatican Council called "the signs of the times" for children in a global consumer culture. We will establish, if only in broad strokes, the situation many of the world's poorest children face and the particular challenges facing even the children of the privileged. It is the task of the church in the modern world to read these signs and interpret them in light of the gospel. In the tradition of Catholic social teaching this call has meant engaging in the process of social analysis. The social sciences are weighing the complex implications of media and advertising to children. There are consequences for children's health and emotional well-being. The logic of the market is influencing many spheres of life, even those previously considered immune from such influence including marriage, family, health care, and education. In this context children are reduced to consumers, commodities, and burdens on family and community.[34] The exploitation of children takes on many forms from dehumanizing child labor, sex work, and soldiering on the one hand to the manipulation of their purchasing power on the other. Information from organizations including UNICEF and the Children's Defense Fund will be incorporated into the task of social analysis. Finally, the impact of a consumer driven society on schools, perhaps the most crucial mediating institutions that serve children, will also be analyzed.

The next movement in the methodological spiral of Catholic social teaching is to judge, to reflect on what we experience in light of Christian commitments. Children are involved in the economic life of their communities; this is a fact. The task may not be to exclude or marginalize children, but rather to shape their involvement according to the norms of justice, taking into account their developmental needs. The response to child exploitation has tended to move in one of two directions: advocating children's rights or promoting family values. Among the latter are parental autonomy and personal responsibility. Chapter 2 will explore these two dominant approaches to seeking the well-being of children. Each in its own way is an answer to the claim that "the market will take care of children." Each approach has strengths and liabilities. Children's rights advocates recognize the individual dignity of children and the claims they can make on their communities for support and protection. Rights language has been open to the charge of embodying the individualism that is a trademark of Western culture and failing to account for children's dependence on families. The debates about family values on the other hand give weight to the autonomy of the family unit and to parental authority. In this context it is possible for children's needs and interests to be obscured or neatly equated with the interests of the family. The family values conversation is also heavily influenced by traditional views of the patriarchal family which may not resonate across cultures, may further marginalize children who are not members of families that fit the mold, and fail to address the particular vulnerabilities of young girls.

In spite of these weaknesses, elements of each approach are crucial if the status of the world's children, especially its poorest children, is to improve. Instruments like the UN *Convention on the Rights of the Child* and other international protocols are vital in assessing the concrete well-being of children and measuring their access to basic needs. The concept of the common good bridges the gap between these two languages, mitigates their liabilities, and provides a fruitful way to address the many issues facing children. It takes concrete well-being seriously, recognizes interdependence as a reality and a good of human community, and expands our vision of solidarity beyond the confines of home toward children everywhere.

Chapter 3 will begin by briefly exploring the tradition of the common good in the social teaching of the church. Basic elements of the concept will be brought to relief: intrinsic human dignity is social and interdependent; there are goods and goals to be pursued beyond those of the individual; these goods are achieved in community; the fruits of social life are to be shared justly; and participation in the building up of those goods is a mark of justice. The concrete requirements of the common good tradition are increasingly shaped by another commitment of the church's social teaching: the option for the poor. This option keeps the common good from being misrepresented as a form of collectivism in which the good of the individual is subordinated to the interest of the group, which often amounts to the interest of those with power and privilege.

That children have an urgent claim on the community's resources is not an especially controversial claim, even though we often fail to answer that claim by providing those resources to the children who need them. Controversies arise when we try to articulate children's participatory role in society. The common good tradition will help us explore the nature of children's social and moral agency. These commitments to children's dignity, full membership in the community, and their participation as moral agents and developing agents of social change will then be brought to bear on the examples of commercialization and consumerism.

Once we see, judge, and reflect on children's well-being in light of our theological traditions, we are called to act. In order to demonstrate the potential for this vision of children and childhood informed by a commitment to the common good to be realized in the concrete, chapter 4 will introduce an example of resistance to and transformation of the logic of the market that welcomes children's participation in the common good. Importantly, this section highlights renewed roles for mediating institutions in securing children's well-being and flourishing. The Cristo Rey Center for the Working Child responded to the need for many children in Peru to work in order to support their families. While it endeavors to end exploitative child labor, the center developed an educational and social services program that incorporates the needs of children who work so that their education need not be the price paid for family survival. Here in the United States, advocates have developed a model for secondary schools that grows out of the experiences of the Cristo Rey Center. These schools incorporate student work as both a way to develop skills and social capital, but also as a way to support the school financially. The young people attending these schools are full participants, striving not only for their own success but also for the maintenance of the school. These models take the market's influence on our lives seriously but aim to shape that influence according to the common good, which includes children as recipients and participants, indeed as brothers and sisters, companions in pursuit of the peaceable kingdom.

Notes

1. Information and excerpts can be found at the UNICEF website, www.UNICEF .org (January 4, 2009).

2. UNICEF, *Children's Forum Message.*

3. Kofi Annan, *Statement at the Opening of the Special Session,* May 8, 2002. Emphasis added. www.unicef.org/specialsession.

4. Annan, *Statement.*

5. Judith M. Gundry-Volf, "The Least and the Greatest: Children in the New Testament," in *The Child in Christian Thought,* ed. Marcia J. Bunge (Grand Rapids, MI: Eerdmans, 2001), 29–60.

6. Thomas Massaro, *Living Justice: Catholic Social Teaching in Action* (Lanham, MD: Sheed & Ward, 2000).

7. International protocols, including the United Nations *Convention on the Rights of the Child,* define a child as a person under the age of eighteen.

8. On the cultural construction of childhood see Philippe Ariès, *L'Enfant et la vie familiale sous l'ancien regime* (Paris: Libraire Plon, 1960), translated by Robert Baldick as *Centuries of Childhood: A Social History of Family Life* (New York: Alfred A. Knopf, 1962); Hugh Cunningham, *Children and Childhood in Western Society Since 1500,* (London and New York: Longman, 1995); and *The Children of the Poor: Representations of Childhood since the 17th Century* (Oxford and Cambridge, MA: Blackwell, 1991); Colin Heywood, *A History of Childhood: Children and Childhood in the West from Medieval to Modern Times* (Cambridge: Polity, 2001); and C. Philip Hwang, Michael E. Lamb, and Irving E. Sigel, eds., *Images of Childhood* (Mahwah, NJ: Lawrence Erlbaum Associates, 1996).

9. Patrick T. McCormick, "Fit to Be Tried?" *America* 186, no. 4 (February 11, 2002): 15–18. The Children's Defense Fund is also drawing attention to the "cradle to prison pipeline" that characterizes the outlook for many African American boys in our urban areas.

10. Donald H. Dunson, *Child, Victim, Soldier: The Loss of Innocence in Uganda* (Maryknoll, NY: Orbis, 2008).

11. Shulamith Shahar, *Childhood in the Middle Ages* (London: Routledge, 1990).

12. Viviana A. Zelizer, *Pricing the Priceless Child: The Changing Social Value of Children* (NY: Basic Books, 1985).

13. Zelizer, *Pricing the Priceless Child*, 11.

14. Zelizer, *Pricing the Priceless Child*, 3.

15. Zelizer, *Pricing the Priceless Child*, 6.

16. Zelizer, *Pricing the Priceless Child*, 52.

17. Maura A. Ryan, *Ethics and Economics of Assisted Reproduction: The Cost of Longing* (Washington, DC: Georgetown University Press, 2001).

18. Jonathan Kozol, *Ordinary Resurrections: Children in the Years of Hope* (New York: Crown Publishers, 2000), 116.

19. Don Browning, *Equality and the Family: A Fundamental Practical Theology of Children, Mothers, and Fathers in Modern Society* (Grand Rapids, MI: Eerdmans, 2007), 4–6. Constructive critiques of Browning's approach with respect to the ethics of family life are found in the companion volume, John Witte Jr., M. Christian Green, and Amy Wheeler, eds., *The Equal Regard Family and Its Friendly Critics: Don Browning and the Practical Theological Ethics of the Family* (Grand Rapids, MI: Eerdmans, 2007).

20. Bonnie J. Miller-McLemore, *Let the Children Come: Reimagining Childhood from a Christian Perspective* (San Francisco: Jossey-Bass, 2003), xxix–xxx.

21. Miller-McLemore, *Let the Children Come*, 74.

22. Miller-McLemore, *Let the Children Come* and *In the Midst of Chaos: Caring for Children as Spiritual Practice* (San Francisco: Jossey-Bass, 2007). With Don S. Browning, Miller-McLemore has recently edited *Children and Childhood in American Religions* (Camden, NJ: Rutgers University Press, 2009).

23. Marcia J. Bunge, ed., *The Child in Christian Thought* (Grand Rapids, MI: Eerdmans, 2001). Bunge, with Terrence E. Fretheim and Beverly Roberts Gaventa, has also recently edited *The Child in the Bible* (Grand Rapids, MI: Eerdmans, 2008).

24. Pamela Couture, *Child Poverty: Love, Justice, and Social Responsibility* (St. Louis, MO: Chalice Press, 2007) and *Seeing Children, Seeing God: A Practical Theology of Children and Poverty* (Nashville, TN: Abingdon Press, 2000).

25. John Wall, "Let the Little Children Come: Child Rearing as Challenge to Christian Ethics," *Horizons* 31, no. 1 (Spring 2004): 64–87.

26. David H. Jensen, *Graced Vulnerability: A Theology of Childhood* (Cleveland: Pilgrim Press, 2005).

27. Pamela K. Brubaker, Rebecca Todd Peters, and Laura A. Stivers, eds., *Justice in a Global Economy* (Louisville, KY: Westminster John Knox, 2006).

28. David Hollenbach, *The Common Good and Christian Ethics* (Cambridge: Cambridge University Press, 2002).

29. Kenneth R. Himes, "Consumerism and Christian Ethics," *Theological Studies* 68 (2007): 132–53 at 133.

30. Himes, "Consumerism and Christian Ethics," 133–34. Citing Alan Aldridge, *Consumption* (Malden, MA: Polity, 2003), 2.

31. Himes, "Consumerism and Christian Ethics," 136–37.

32. Himes, "Consumerism and Christian Ethics," 149.

33. Schor, Juliet. "The Commodification of Childhood: Tales from the Advertising Front Lines," *Hedgehog Review* 5, no. 2 (2003): 7–23.

34. Todd David Whitmore with Tobias Winright, "Children: An Undeveloped Theme in Catholic Teaching," in *The Challenge of Global Stewardship: Roman Catholic Responses*, ed. Maura A. Ryan and Todd David Whitmore (Notre Dame, IN: Notre Dame University Press, 1997), 161–85.

1

Reading the Signs of the Times

Consumer Culture and the Commercialization of Childhood

The story we tell can never replace the child. It can only replace the silence.

—Danna Nolan Fewell[1]

Two Childhoods

A JUNIOR HIGH SCHOOL STUDENT IN A SUBURB of Toronto, a child of relative privilege, Craig Kielburger, woke one morning to an image on the front page of the newspaper of a young man, Iqbal Masih, who had been killed in Lahore, Pakistan.[2] Unbeknownst to Craig, Iqbal had been featured in the press as a symbol of the tragedy of child labor for children's rights activists. Iqbal was one of the lucky few who had been liberated from his bonded labor in a carpet factory. He had been "sold" into bonded labor at the age of four and freed by the Bonded Labour Liberation Front at the age of ten.[3] He had been honored with the Reebok Youth in Action Human Rights Award in 1994 and was quickly known worldwide as a victim of the exploitation of children and as a symbol of hope for change.

Tanya Roberts-Davis paints a portrait of life in a carpet factory drawn from her conversations with children involved in the RugMark program in South East Asia:

Imagine waking up at 5 o'clock every morning to start work in a dimly lit carpet factory. Sitting on a hard wooden bench in front of a loom, your job is to quickly tie knots that you then tighten with a heavy toothed hammer. The only windows in the building are small and placed near the ceiling. There are bars across them. At times, you can hear the laughter of school children outside. You continue to weave until nine o'clock at night. You have only two short meal breaks. . . . There is time for just one trip to the toilet. The air is thick with dust from the wool, which gets into your lungs, making your chest ache when you breathe.[4]

The conditions under which children work in the carpet factories are appalling to be sure. Additionally, any mistakes they make in the work incur penalties that make it impossible to repay their debt. They sit hunched over for long periods which impact their proper development and require physical rehabilitation once they are liberated. Many children are also subjected to beatings and sexual abuse.

Back in Canada, Craig was moved by the newspaper story and set out to find out more about Iqbal, child labor, and what he could do about it. He embarked on a journey that would lead him across Asia to visit with working children and those who had been liberated. Together with other students in Canada, Craig founded Free the Children, an organization dedicated to ending child labor and building bridges between children throughout the world. He has reflected on the need to have children participate in social life, while at the same time protecting them from abuse. As a teenager he became passionate about the issue of exploitative child labor in many parts of the world and his research into the issue presented two contrasting challenges:

In many developing countries, children are often asked to work long hours at hazardous jobs with no opportunity to play or go to school. They are not allowed to develop physically, intellectually, and emotionally as they should. They support entire families. They fight in wars. They are given too much responsibility at too young an age. . . . On the other hand, in many industrialized countries everything is done for children. They are segregated most of their lives with members of their own age group and are given little opportunity to assume a social conscience, or to learn through interaction with adults. Through media they learn to be consumers, to gain their self-image through the electronic toys they own and the labels they wear. They too, are exploited. They see violence and suffering on the news every day but are told that they are too young to do anything about it. They are conditioned to become passive bystanders. . . . We want to help free children from both extremes.[5]

His insights into the lives of poor children and the lives of his peers are powerful. There is no middle ground between those children who have been pressed into great responsibility at staggering personal cost, and those children who are shielded not only from the harshest forms of exploitation but from any meaningful participation as well. That there might be a connection between the lives of privilege enjoyed by some children and the abject poverty experienced by others is rarely considered in public debate. The particular experiences had by Craig, his peers, and the children in the carpet factories provide a window onto the many forms of exploitation and marginalization faced by children worldwide.

A Global Picture

In the opening paragraphs of the Second Vatican Council's encyclical, *Gaudium et Spes, The Church in the Modern World,* Christians, and indeed all people of good will are called on to read the signs of the times and interpret them in light of the gospel.[6] As Christians and all people of good will strive to fashion what the United Nations has called "a world fit for children" we must ask, what are the signs of the times for children?[7] What are the moral, social, and economic forces that not only threaten their future, but undermine children's human dignity in the present? And then, how might these forces be counteracted or directed in ways that advance human dignity and relationships?

In the United States, and in much of the world, church communities are still reeling from the sex abuse scandal. Terrible violations of the dignity of children and young people have been perpetrated over the course of decades by members of the clergy and others involved in the pastoral care or education of children. This tragedy was compounded by actions taken on the part of those in power to cover up the abuse and shield the abusers and the institutions of the church. The reaction on the part of the hierarchy betrayed a profound ambiguity in the church's attitudes toward children and their intrinsic dignity.

First, we can note that the controversy only erupted when allegations were made public by victims who were by that time adult men. People were horrified by the abuse of children, but the issues that received abundant attention in the wake of initial allegations were homosexuality, the nature of pedophilia as an illness, the vocation to celibacy, a culture of secrecy in the church, and the abuse of authority among those entrusted to pastor the People of God. As victims sought redress through the courts, the financial impact of settlements took center stage as dioceses declared bankruptcy and closed parishes and schools. At issue was the need for fiscal accountability and transparency as well as an increased role for lay adults in church governance, particularly in financial matters. All of these issues demanded thoughtful attention and careful study in order to address the crisis in a comprehensive manner.

Consequently, the United States bishops issued directives to protect children in parish and parochial school settings.[8] These included a number of practical, commonsense strategies about background checks on ministers, teachers, coaches, and volunteers, including parents. Dioceses have initiated various training programs for adults and for children about how to identify, report, and perhaps most importantly prevent and resist abusive situations. These were crucial steps, however limited they might be. What did not receive needed attention was a broader and deeper examination of the culture's use of children as objects, including objects of sexual desire, in advertising and entertainment media—and the ways in which that culture influences attitudes within the church. Neither did we entertain a sustained conversation about adolescent sexuality. In the parochial school my children attended, some parents were wary of abuse prevention programs thinking that they might introduce children to sexual issues in spite of the fact that training is largely about personal safety. The danger here is that some children, in order to be protected from anything "sexual," were also not made aware of strategies and skills they could use to protect themselves in any number of threatening situations. Attention also needed to be paid to if, when, and how we listen to children, their experiences, and how they and we interpret those experiences. These child-centered issues were rarely in the headlines of theological and ethical debate.

This dark episode in the church's history has rightly received legal, legislative, and media attention. What had been hidden, festering, needed to come to light. While addressing the complexity of the sexual abuse of children within church settings, and the sexual abuse and exploitation of children generally, is beyond the scope of this project, the abuse crisis is necessarily part of the atmosphere in which Christians, Catholic Christians in particular, address children's well-being and advocate on their behalf. Rhetoric about our care for children must be matched not only with concrete practices of justice and compassion, but also with genuine repentance and desire for reconciliation that reaches deeply into the corridors of clerical power and broadly to include all members of the Christian community who, however unwittingly, contribute to children's vulnerability. As the church strives to be a countercultural witness to the gospel, we must examine our complicity in the wider culture's denigration of children. It is my sincere hope that the church's credibility on these questions has not been irreparably damaged.

Our present focus on children's participation in the economic life of their communities and the vulnerability they experience in this sphere demands that we bracket our just concerns about their sexual exploitation and the particularly complex task of addressing that with the necessary nuance. That being said, these two issues are not easily distinguished; we need only think

of advertising that portrays children as sexual objects, that promotes provocative clothing to young girls, the trade in child pornography, the sexual
harassment and abuse of children in work settings, and the children involved
in the global sex trade. Harm done to children in churches and church related
environments occurs in this broader context and so attention to this form of
abuse necessarily draws us deeper into an analysis of consumer culture and
the many intersecting and overlapping forms of children's exploitation. It is
to these concerns that we now turn, reading the "signs of the times" of which
the sex abuse crisis is but one glaring manifestation.

The Children's Defense Fund (CDF) and the United Nations Children's
Fund (UNICEF) publish annual assessments of the state of the world's children along a number of different axes. Children are especially vulnerable to the
ravages of poverty, violence, disease, malnutrition, and environmental devastation. When these arise in contexts all too often shaped by sexism, racism, and
religious or ethnic conflict, the situation becomes even more critical.

The CDF, founded in the United States by children's advocate Marian
Wright Edelman, sponsors an institute each year for those engaged in child
advocacy ministry. Their 2004 program booklet opens, "If we believe that
children are created in the image of God, then how well are we tending the
image of the One who created us?" The answer: not well at all. In the United
States each day 4 children are killed by abuse and neglect, 8 children or teens
are killed by firearms, 76 babies die before their first birthday, 366 children are
arrested for drug abuse, 1,707 babies are born without health insurance, and
2,171 babies are born into poverty.[9] The statistics should be sobering for citizens of one of the wealthiest and most powerful nations in the world. Other
statistics reveal a very different set of national priorities. Among industrialized
nations, the United States ranks first in military technology, military exports,
gross domestic product, in numbers of millionaires and billionaires, in health
technology and defense expenditures.[10]

In the United States, one in three children will be poor at some point in
childhood, one in five is born poor, and one in five children under the age of
three years is poor right now.[11] Only one in seven children eligible for federal
child care assistance receives it, and two in five children eligible for Head Start
do not participate. One child in eight has no health insurance. One child in
fourteen children lives at less than half of the poverty level. And 1 in every 146
children dies before their first birthday.[12] These statistics are scandalous for
a country that is arguably the richest and most powerful in the world, both
politically and economically.[13] When we turn to the developing world, the
situation for children becomes even worse.

UNICEF provides mountains of statistical information on children's well-
being in a global perspective. UNICEF argues for "a human rights-based,

multisectoral approach to development."[14] UNICEF's "key priorities" for children include child protection, immunization, early childhood, fighting HIV/AIDS, and girls' education. The picture that UNICEF paints of the lives of the world's poorest children is bleak:

> Hundreds of millions of children across the globe are victims of exploitation, abuse and violence each year. They are abducted from their homes and schools and recruited into the army. They are trafficked into prostitution rings. They are forced into debt bondage or other forms of slavery.[15]

Some of the statistics include 246 million children in exploitative child labor (5.7 million of whom work in "especially horrific circumstances"). We have already encountered these children in the person of Iqbal Masih and the children of RugMark. Over one million children are involved in the commercial sex industry. Three hundred thousand children as young as eight years of age are soldiers engaged in armed conflict in over thirty countries. In the past decade, two million children died in armed conflict and six million more have been seriously injured or permanently disabled (eight to ten thousand of who have been killed or injured by landmines). Thirty million children do not receive immunizations, resulting in two million unnecessary deaths. Eleven million children (30,000 per day) die before the age of five years. Of these eleven million, four million die in their first month of life.[16] The root causes of these statistics are many and often involve a confluence of factors; debate rages over just what to do in order to address them.

These statistics provide important evidence of the reality of children's lives that moves us beyond the anecdotal. Unfortunately, statistics and staggering numbers can be mind numbing and heart hardening. Thankfully, advocates like Donald Dunson have undertaken to show us the human face of poverty and exploitation in the lives of children. This is dangerous business. Dunson shares his trepidation on visiting child soldiers in Uganda:

> But I did fear for my soul. My new, first hand knowledge of the plight of these extremely vulnerable children would bear vast moral consequences. I felt ill prepared to assume them.[17]

Of his meeting with Sunday Obote, a former child soldier, he writes,

> After the first minutes of our conversation I knew that I had never looked into the eyes of someone so young and so wounded as this teenager. Nor had I ever met a youth so familiar with killing.[18]

The narratives in Dunson's *No Room at the Table: Earth's Most Vulnerable Children*, introduce us to Carlos, a ten-year-old Salvadoran boy who supports his family by selling water; to Siri, a young Thai girl sold into prostitution; and to Juliet, a housemaid at thirteen in Uganda, lured to this work with the never met promise of education.[19] He recounts his powerful encounters with these children and brings their voices to those of us who may be far away, but who can no longer claim not to know the human cost of exploitation and still "be true to our best selves."[20] As we continue with our ethical analysis, we must take the risk that comes with knowing, or at least knowing about, the world's poorest children, keeping both the statistical information and the personal human narratives at the beginning our hermeneutical spiral.

While many of the statistics from UNICEF and the CDF refer to children as a group in themselves, it must be noted that children are also members of already marginalized groups and so many of these conditions are shaped as much by race, gender, and socioeconomic status as they are by age. Though all children are vulnerable to negative economic forces, the nature of that vulnerability and the ways in which it manifests itself can vary greatly between poor children and children of economic privilege (which often goes hand in hand with racial and gender privilege). In what follows we will explore two extremes of children's participation in the economic life of their families and communities: child labor, which brings the plight of poor children into stark relief, and children as consumers, which highlights the dangers faced by non-poor children.

The Dominance of the Market as Mechanism and Metaphor

While much of the suffering endured by the world's children arises from a number of interacting factors, it cannot be denied that the spread of global market capitalism plays a key role especially as it relates to root causes of injustice in poverty. While advocates claim that free markets hold the key to the successful distribution of the world's resources and to development among peoples, the expansion of markets seems to have brought prosperity to a relative few at the expense of many.

Markets have their own logic and language: supply, demand, free entry, rational choice, promotion of self-interest (however "enlightened" that interest might be), the maximization of profit and the minimization of risk. Markets can be an effective way to distribute goods but there is little if anything in the logic of the market itself to secure a measure of equality or guard against the exploitation of some who cannot exercise the same freedoms as those in places of privilege and power. Children figure largely in this exploited population. Neither the advantages of profit nor the burdens of risk are equally shared. This has become painfully clear as major corporations fail, and employees and shareholders suffer while executives walk away from the debris with millions of dollars.

It has been argued persuasively that the market's role in the distribution of some goods of social living should be extremely limited if not eliminated. One example receiving much needed attention is the health care market. If access to health care is a basic human right, then it cannot be left to the whims of the market to provide that access to all people irrespective of their ability to pay for it. Controversies over access to pharmaceuticals, particularly in the countries of the developing world struggling under the crushing weight of HIV, AIDS, tuberculosis, and malaria, have prompted discussions about the limits of the market, the regulation of industries, trade agreements, and patent law.[21]

The dominance of the market has brought on a proliferation of market metaphors and philosophical assumptions into areas of social life that had heretofore been considered immune from the market's cold calculations—the family and educational institutions figure among these. The following sections will explore several axes along which children participate in the market as a means of distributing goods and services and also the ways in which children are impacted by the expansion of consumerism.

Children's Labor and Work

Chief among the ways in which many of the world's children are active in the market is through their labor. Our reading of the signs of the times for children revealed staggering numbers of children who are engaged in wage labor—much of it in "especially horrific circumstances." Iqbal Masih's story in Pakistan stands as one example of factory labor in dehumanizing conditions and undertaken to satisfy a family debt rather than for a wage. The phenomenon of child labor is complex and is more of a global problem (including countries in the industrialized north) than we might first realize.

In the United States, as in other industrialized nations of the northern hemisphere, child labor is viewed primarily as a problem of the developing world and there are periodic bursts of outrage when it is discovered that consumer goods purchased here have been produced in factories that employ children in other parts of the world. Unfortunately some of this outrage is prompted by celebrity involvement in the scandal rather than sought after knowledge about the status of the world's children. Child labor as a social problem may be part of our history, but surely not part of our present. One researcher in Britain noted that when asked about child labor, respondents referred to existing legislation that prevents abuse and monitors the conditions of children who work. Most people articulated some widely held assumptions: that child work is a minority experience; it involves "light tasks" deemed appropriate for children; and that existing legislation effectively controls child labor practices. To the limited extent that children work, the portrait of that work is idealized.[22]

And yet, our culture is caught in the middle of some conflicting emotions: "American parents, policymakers, and pundits worry continuously over the work ethic of the next generation and believe in the importance of instilling responsibility and good work habits. But child labor is seen as something that happens to other people in some other place or time."[23] So Americans can at the same time raise an alarm about child labor abroad, and also lament that youth employment, or underemployment, is a critical problem on the home front. As the summer nears, public policy makers seek to encourage local businesses to provide employment opportunities for youth, particularly those in the inner city. This often builds on the rhetoric that idle hands are the devil's workshop. Work by some children is thereby also viewed as a way to prevent social ills like crime and teenage pregnancy.

It is surely the case that exploitative child labor is a problem in poorer countries, as indicated in reports from UNICEF, but it remains an issue in the United States as well. According to historian Hugh Hindman, "As America enters the twenty-first century, children continue to work, but the mix of industries, occupations, hours, and conditions for most working children has changed so dramatically that much of this work is no longer defined as a child labor problem."[24] The exceptions made for agriculture are probably the most striking. The iconic image of the family farm, emblematic of American self sufficiency and connection to nature has shaped public policy in this area with respect to children's involvement. For Hindman, this is a failure of policy to protect children's interests: "In contrast with most other sectors, the minimum age for employment in agriculture is twelve, and there are no restrictions on hours. While estimates are grossly imprecise, it is clear there are hundreds of thousands of children under sixteen working as hired agricultural laborers."[25]

Americans' belief that we no longer have a child labor problem is a historical development, and one furthered by misrepresentations in the statistical data on employment:

> By 1930, the labor forces participation of ten-to-fourteen-year-olds had fallen to 5.56 percent. Thereafter we stopped counting gainful workers under fourteen and stopped tracking labor force activity of these youngsters. From a data perspective, this aspect of the child labor problem disappeared.
>
> Similarly, labor force activity rates of fourteen- and fifteen-year-olds peaked at 30.9 percent in 1900 and, by 1940, had declined to 5.2 percent. After 1967, the

Department of Labor changed the definition of the U.S. labor force, restricting it to those aged sixteen or older, and we stopped counting fourteen- and fifteen-year-olds. The remainder of America's child labor problem was purged from the quantitative record. Anecdotal accounts of child labor abuses could be dismissed as exceptional.[26]

Children have disappeared from the data and so have disappeared from our deliberations about labor, just remuneration and working conditions. The logic seems somewhat circular: if we define laborers or workers as those above the age of sixteen and only maintain data on this category, then there is no record of a child labor "problem"; if we have no data then there are, de facto, no laborers under the age of sixteen—no problem. We avoid careful analysis of any systemic challenges and are then able to view abuse as something isolated and rectifiable one incident at a time. We treat symptoms without acknowledging any underlying pathology.

Another arena of child labor in industrialized nations that needs very careful examination is work done by another hidden group: undocumented immigrants. Young people with their families as well as unaccompanied minors have been found in Immigration and Customs Enforcement (ICE) raids here in the United States. While the impact of immigration on the economy often focuses on adults who come to the United States to work and to send money home to their country of origin, it is also the case that some children do the same. In other parts of the world many children also migrate within their home countries, moving from rural areas to urban centers in search of work which often results in their exploitation.[27]

As we move through an analysis of the phenomenon of child labor, we begin to notice an important operating distinction being made between child labor and child work. "Child labor" carries with it the connotation of exploitation and abuse. This is labor that is hazardous, undertaken for extremely low or no wages, and comes at the expense of a child's education and growth. This labor is almost always linked with poverty and unfortunately, some of the blame for this phenomenon often falls on parents who are portrayed as willing to sacrifice their children out of greed.[28]

"Child work" is usually intended as a morally neutral term, free of the negative connotations associated with "labor." The description offered by Hindman of the work done by children and youth that is admired in the United States—in a somewhat self-congratulatory way on the part of parents—is remarkably different from labor:

> These are jobs that may be expected to foster responsibility, dependability, punctuality, and self-confidence, traits presumed to have positive effects on future endeavors whether at work or at school. Further, the data suggest that much of this

work is performed within household and communal networks where children perform paid services for their parents, relatives, and their parents' friends and neighbors. A greater portion of white children than black children hold freelance jobs and the likelihood of freelance job-holding increases as parental income increases. One of today's main concerns is that blacks and other economically disadvantaged youngsters are disproportionately deprived of opportunities to gain valuable work experience. That this is an important concern suggests just how much the qualitative nature of the phenomenon has changed.[29]

This description requires careful analysis on a number of different levels. First, it is the paper route, lawn mowing, babysitting, or office gofer that comes to mind since the work is done primarily within the community of people who are known to the child and her family. The nature of this is quite different from factory wage labor. Second, this form of child work is not linked to poverty. In fact, just the opposite is often the case. The wealthier the child, the more likely she is to been involved in this type of employment. Third, the benefits of employment redound primarily to the child in the form of character building. The income is not a crucial aspect of the family's economy let alone needed for basic survival. Income is likely spent by the child on a new video game, iPod, or some other latest fad. Such economic involvement conveys something about the "value" of money and about having earned one's way. This education about money also draws on American admiration for an imagined self-sufficiency: I have what I have because I deserve it and because I earned it on my own. Finally, this is "after school" work; school and health concerns usually trump these responsibilities when there is a conflict. Suburban America is no stranger to the sight of a parent finishing the paper route because there is homework to be done or a flu going around.

A solid character and diligent work ethic (and the occasional new toy) are not the only benefits of such employment reaped on the part of young people. This work is had by young people whose parents have not only financial resources, but social capital as well.[30] This social capital is then extended to the child and becomes increasingly important in the pursuit of higher education and adult employment. This accounts for the desire on the part of some child advocates to ensure that employment opportunities are open to poor children and children of color. These are the un- or underemployed young people who do not benefit from the social capital garnered by children of privilege in the form of school and business connections and letters of reference. Sadly, the public rhetoric tends to play the fear card more often than it advocates justice for young people: poor children of color who do not find after-school and summer employment pose a threat to the safety and security of the community.

Another underside to some efforts to provide work (including work as a volunteer) noted by Kiku Adatto in "Selling Out Childhood," is that children

become "living résumés." Important contributions are those that happen outside of the home rather than within the family network (for example, being a
nursing home volunteer counts more than visiting your grandmother, being
a tutor more than caring for younger siblings) and valuable relationships are
those that can be understood in market terms.[31]

So we come to the contemporary situation out of a history fraught with
paradox that continues: children should be immune from the world of work
in order to enjoy childhood; children should be able to work in contexts that
are safe and do not threaten education and health in order to instill civic
virtues. Unfortunately, neither of these positions on its own adequately addresses the situation of child work as it takes shape globally. The tension does
however point to the need for a framework to think about how children can
participate in relationships that serve their well-being and the well-being of
others.

Because citizens of northern industrialized countries view exploitative
labor as a problem in the "third world," the rhetoric tends toward rescue, as it
did with the chimney sweeps of another era. Well meaning attempts at rescue
or liberation on the grounds that all child labor should be eliminated have
notoriously backfired as children are forced into worse situations—including
sex work—when factories have been shut down in response to consumer outrage in the United States. The many intersecting factors that impact children's
well-being are rarely considered. Even those who demand the elimination of
child labor sometimes do so with motives other than the best interests of the
children themselves. For example, resolutions adopted by the International
Labour Conference in June 2008 regarding children involved in agricultural
work (which is exempt from minimum age regulations) claim, "Child labour
undermines decent work, and the effective functioning of rural labour markets is undermined by the presence of child labour." Concerns about the potential for this to deepen poverty are real and legitimate. However, we need to
question frameworks that pit the interests of adult workers against children.
This has led to demands on the part of organizations of child workers to a
right to work in order to provide for themselves and their families.[32]

Exploitative labor of any kind is violation of basic human dignity and
children are particularly vulnerable. For many poor families and children,
child work is essential to survival and a manifestation of faithfulness to family obligations and so our moral language about work, even work involving
children must be complex enough to challenge injustice and yet leave space
for children's participation in this vital aspect of social life. We will see that
the language of the common good within Catholic social teaching, with an
emphasis on rights and responsibilities, has this required nuance.

"Little Spenders"

Another sign of our times is the multimillion dollar advertising industry aimed at reaching children and young people as consumers. This is the context that Craig Kielburger noticed influencing his peers and occupying a greater portion of their self-understanding (feeling empowered as consumers but powerless to effect any real change in their communities). Increasingly, children and young people have become the direct targets, a description chosen deliberately, of intense advertising campaigns. It could be argued that many products advertised to children as consumers and as key players in their families' spending habits do not necessarily undermine their well-being in any inordinate way—the latest minivan or the family trip to a theme park for example. Many critics are primarily concerned with the *content* of programming and advertising and focus on the marketing of sex, violence, alcohol, and tobacco, and the incorporation of these into characters, games and clothing. Others are alerting us to the corrosive effects of advertising itself on the bodies and spirits of children and young people today.

The cover of the fall 2004 issue of *Boston College Magazine* displayed a colorful image of the Mall of America in Bloomington, Minnesota. The caption read, "Hey, little spenders: The seduction of America's children." The magazine featured an article by sociology professor Juliet Schor entitled "America's Most Wanted: Inside the World of Young Consumers."[33] One of her opening statistics is startling: "American children view an estimated 40,000 commercials annually."[34] Schor is raising the alarm about the overwhelming presence of advertising in the lives of children and young people.

Citing James McNeal, author of *Kids as Customers: A Handbook of Marketing to Children*, Schor claims that children aged four through twelve made $6.1 billion in purchases in 1989, $23.4 billion in 1997, and $30 billion in 2002, which represents an increase of 400 percent.[35] Children comprise a huge and very lucrative market in the United States. They purchase food, toys, clothing, electronics, and increasingly have a say in decisions about other major family expenditures such as cars and vacations. Companies attempt to secure brand loyalty at younger and younger ages by initiating children to a product line even when the products are intended for older children and young adults. Scholars like Schor and Susan Linn stress the negative impact of advertising media itself on children's health and well-being even though the actual content of the media should also come under scrutiny for violence and sexually explicit material.[36]

Susan Linn in her book, *Consuming Kids: The Hostile Takeover of Childhood*, relates the experience of attending a conference for marketing professionals who target children.[37] While the attendees seemed enthusiastic and well-meaning, Linn notes that no one ever questioned whether the ads or the products themselves were *good* for children. The ethics of manipulating children's emotions in order to convince them they need a certain style of clothing or brand of shampoo was never discussed. No one questioned or critiqued the means of obtaining information about children, a practice that has become increasingly invasive. Market researchers enter children's homes, often with video camera in hand, and observe the children's behaviors in the most private places in the home, the bedrooms and bathrooms.[38] Schor notes that "researchers can make the claim that they know children in ways that are far deeper, more sophisticated, and more profound than a past generation that relied on focus groups and standard surveys did."[39]

While children are protected as participants in all sorts of medical research (through provisions for informed consent that include information about potential risks to well-being), there are no such protections in market research in the United States.[40] Protections in market research are often limited to permission slips or forms of "passive consent," where parents must object to their child's participation in a study. Though permission forms offer some protection for children, they do not address the potential conflict of interest between parents and children particularly when there is a financial incentive to participate in a research study. According to Schor,

> Parents have a financial incentive to use their kids in these ways and have the right to force them to participate even if they'd prefer not to. And even if the children enjoy it, one has to ask whether it's really in their interest.[41]

Why might the children enjoy participating in these research protocols or marketing tactics? For researchers the answer is simple. Apart from the lure of "free stuff," researchers have created a space where the child's opinions and desires count. Marketing firms have painted a picture of the world in which parents and teachers "are not paying attention or empowering kids."[42] It is the ad agencies and those who employ them who are willing to listen to children and then act on the child's advice.[43] This is the "kid-centric" approach. A *kid* is not a *child*. Children are innocent; kids are savvy and streetwise while their parents are hopelessly "clueless."

Some of the research done into children's habits of consuming has revealed the powerful presence of "the nag factor," familiar to anyone with young children. Picture a parent and child in the grocery store in the candy aisle (which is now conveniently the aisle featuring granola bars and other marginally healthier snack items). The child sees the candy, asks for the candy, asks loudly, pleads loudly with tears, and finally ends with an all-out tantrum. At some point in this drama, the parent acquiesces if only to keep the child quiet, and to avoid embarrassment before the other shoppers. In one sense, the child has become an agent of the corporation, manipulating the parent into making certain purchases irrespective of their value for the child or the family.[44]

Marketing professionals no longer need to market to the parents who make purchases on behalf of their children. Ads that sought to convince parents that a product is good for their children or will make them happy are giving way to ads directed at children themselves. Children simply need to make repeated and repeated requests for a particular product. A parent can say no only so many times. The nag factor is almost inescapable, making the need to sway mom and dad directly almost negligible.

That is not to say that mom and dad are out of the picture altogether. A growing number of ads aim at promising parents brighter, more successful children with the purchase of educational computer software or a visit to a for-profit learning and tutoring center. Parents may understand the persuasive intent of the commercials and yet may continue to wonder whether or not there is something more they could be or should be doing to help their child achieve in a competitive atmosphere.

Other researchers are encouraging marketing executives to shift their strategy from reliance on the nag factor toward appealing to the "new super consumer":

> We're here to say that the best way to mom's heart is through—*her children.* Whether she has an infant, kid, tween, or teen, a mom today wants to be the best mom she can possibly be for that child and that means an awful lot of what she does, what she buys, and what she demands of her family is centered around her children.[45]

Mothers and children have become "partners in consumerism." A mother's self-esteem becomes bound up in achieving her children's happiness, which in turn is achieved through purchasing. Mothers in this view also see themselves as teachers in the process of consuming. One mother quoted in the research boasts about her daughter, "She is a pretty savvy little shopper at three."[46] The researchers are almost giddy in their enthusiasm for this claim:

> So strong is this consumer relationship—this partnership—that we see kid and mom as one, virtually joined at the hip, one "Four-Eyed, Four-Legged" consumer—a Super Consumer capable of affecting the purchase of more than $1 trillion in U.S. goods and services every year![47]

Advertisers know how to manipulate and exploit the nag factor and the super consumer. If a product is attractive enough to children, it does not need to meet certain parental requirements. Even though she does not want the child to have the product, eventually the nagging will wear down even the most resistant parent. So children increasingly see ads for products that are not explicitly intended for them or do not serve their well-being in any meaningful way, and may in fact be harmful. The response of the advertisers is familiar: parents should "just say no." The assumption is that parents have complete control over their children's access to media and their spending. Schor is quick to point out just how disingenuous this advice is:

> Many advertisers speak with a forked tongue about parental responsibility. To the public they extol it. To their clients, they boast about their ability to exploit parental weakness.[48]

Writing about those marketing violent video games to young people, David Walsh notes,

> They are only asking themselves if they will sell and create profits. In their private lives, I would expect that many of these same people are parents who are concerned about what is good for their own children. But as part of a larger anonymous group creating violent video entertainment, such concerns are out of place. A creator of a violent video game might not let his or her own child play it, but even if this is the case, there is no sense of responsibility to the millions of other children who will. If the potential for profit is large enough, the game will be produced, regardless of its effect on children.[49]

It is Schor's experience that most parents do indeed take responsibility for their children, for what children do and for what they desire. They are not abdicating this responsibility, however, "most don't think they should be forced to fight the battle alone, and there is strong support for restrictions on advertising."[50] Susan Linn echoes this point when she writes, "Even while I, like all American parents, am held responsible for the behavior of my child and for safeguarding her future, corporations bombard her with messages that undermine my efforts."[51] It seems nearly impossible for individual parents, and even small groups of parents, to successfully resist the efforts of a multibillion dollar marketing industry. The "just say no" strategy is entirely inadequate as a means to safeguard the harmful effects of advertising on young people.

Others have a harsher appraisal of parental attitudes in a consumer culture: "Eyes shut, many parents in this media age hand off their children as if they were cars at a car wash. . . . They relinquish their children unthinkingly to anyone who comes over the airwaves. The process of parental acquiescence happens so gradually that it is hardly detectable."[52] These criticisms locate primary responsibility with parents who should be actively moderating all of their children's access to media and other elements of popular culture. The emphasis shifts away from social or corporate responsibility.

There is "parental peer pressure" that pulls parents in conflicting directions. On the one hand, happy children—the fruit of being a good parent—require the trappings that are part and parcel of consumer culture. So the pressure to acquire consumer goods for one's children is very real. And yet paradoxically,

> everyone knows that alarm about popular culture is part of what goes under the rubric "being a good parent" in America today, hence parent's tendency to underreport the number of hours their children spend watching television and to over report the control they exercise over their children's viewing habits.[53]

Schor and Linn believe that there are indeed serious harmful effects of advertising. The ad culture works to undermine children's well-being along several indices. While advertising is surely not the sole cause of many of the problems facing children in our culture, it cannot be discounted as a contributing factor. Schor names increased instances of childhood depression, anxiety, low self-esteem and psychosomatic symptoms among children with a high exposure to consumer culture.[54] Linn puts the point even more strongly: "Every aspect of children's lives—their physical and mental health, their education, their creativity, and their values—is negatively affected by their involuntary status as consumers in the marketplace."[55]

The claim here is that the media keeps children (and adults) in a constant state of dissatisfaction while at the same time promising to relieve that dissatisfaction by introducing a new "must have" product. Ironically, some of what is marketed to children and young people, violent video games for example, has a desensitizing impact. The focus is often on the fear that the next generation will have no emotional reaction to violence and death or will have a pleasurable reaction since violence has become entertaining. What receives less attention is a desensitization that runs even deeper: no awe, wonder, joy, desire, or real sorrow—profound human experiences that children had once called to our attention.

Similarly, David Walsh highlights the values of the consumer marketplace: happiness is found in having things; get all you can for yourself; get it all as quickly as you can; win at all costs; violence is entertaining; always seek pleasure and avoid boredom. These he juxtaposes with justice/fairness, respect for self and others, cooperation, self-esteem, self-discipline, altruism, generosity, moderation, peaceful conflict resolution, empathy, tolerance/understanding, and social responsibility.[56] Consumerism, the maximization of choice, and ever-upward mobility—our "way of life"—is often at odds with the values we claim to espouse as Americans and even more so as Christians. Yet many of us see no inconsistency between our moral values and dominant cultural values and practices.

While Schor points to psychological effects, others are highlighting the dramatic increase in childhood obesity and diabetes (due to junk food and soft drink consumption) which are reaching epidemic proportions in the United States. Still others might point to deaths and injuries due to violence, and instances of sexual activity, sexually transmitted diseases, and pregnancy among children and young people as harmful outcomes of a media culture that glamorizes sex and violence.[57] In any case, it is becoming clear that the consequences of this consumer culture and advertising to children are not limited to overspending on the part of parents but include real threats to children's physical, emotional, and spiritual well-being.

Under increasing scrutiny is the amount of advertising on behalf of food and beverage industries. According to one study cited in *Food Marketing to Children and Youth,*

> the prevailing pattern of food and beverage products marketed to children and youth has been high in total calories, sugar, salt, fat, and low in nutrients. A dietary profile that mirrors the products marketed would put our children and youth at risk for the types of nutritional problems that we see occurring today—increasing rates of obesity, and inadequacies of certain important micronutrients—and for the development of various serious chronic diseases later in life.[58]

The health implications of this trend are becoming increasingly clear: "More than 9 million U.S. children and youth are obese and another 15 percent are at risk for becoming obese. The prevalence of type 2 diabetes among children and youth—previously known as 'adult-onset' diabetes—has more than doubled in the last decade."[59] If not the health of children as a good in itself, then the looming prospects of the cost of health care for these young people as they grow is prompting action in some sectors.

The study acknowledges right at the outset that "marketing works." The conclusions do not call for a limit to the amount of advertising aimed at children nor does it challenge the image of the child as consumer. Rather, the authors seem to proceed on the assumption that since marketing works, it should be harnessed rather than limited. Successful advertising strategies ought to be marshaled in favor of advertising healthy eating habits and physical exercise. It would appear that these efforts rely on the good will of advertisers and the corporations they serve. Ultimately, these corporations have a fiduciary obligation to their shareholders to maximize profits. The report doesn't address the possible need to compel certain practices. Some have astutely pointed out that it would be difficult to include a toy with an apple or a bunch of grapes.

Lest we think that the reach of consumer culture and its deleterious effects is limited to the United States, in the same way we are tempted to locate the issues of child labor elsewhere in the world, marketing expert James McNeal notes,

> The U.S. model of consumption, in general, has become the guiding model of new consumers the world over, suggesting great market opportunity for many existing U.S. products and brands. . . . Most of the world's population and wealth is outside of the U.S., and both are increasing more rapidly than they are domestically . . . there is ten times as much market potential among children in the rest of the developed and developing world.[60]

Education in Consumer Culture

Commercialization affects education in the United States in a number of different but connected ways. Those who are concerned about the impact that media saturated with commercials is having on children face another, perhaps even more daunting challenge: commercialism in the school system. As Juliet Schor puts it, "The jewel in the marketers' crown of commercial infiltration has been the nation's public schools."[61] There is a growing confidence in the market to provide all of children's needs, including education. Though having well-educated children and young people benefits the common good, many feel that reducing or removing the state's role in providing education would benefit children. An example of this line of thinking was articulated in a recent editorial in the *Boston Globe*:

> There is nothing indispensable about a state role in education. Parents don't expect the government to provide their children's food or clothing or medical care; there is no reason why it must provide their schooling. An educated citizenry is a vital public good, of course. But like most such goods, a competitive and responsive private sector can do a much better job of supplying it than the public sector.[62]

The argument is that the market would provide much needed diversity in education that would respond to the desires of children and parents and would allow for more creativity on the part of teachers. The market-based approach is clearly in view and gaining political popularity. What the editorial fails to mention is that this diversity is already available for families who can pay for it. There are schools that focus on the arts or the sciences, or that emphasize athletics. There are religious and secular schools and those that offer single-sex or coeducation. Many families can't afford to pay for these choices. Moreover, many poor families, poor working families, do rely on the government to help them feed, clothe, house, and provide medical care for their children. The market does play a huge factor in how these goods are distributed in our capitalist economy and it has not provided each and every child in this country with adequate food, clothing, housing, and health care. Millions of children are left behind; their basic needs have not been provided by the free market. There is no reason to suspect that the same would not also be true of education. Many children might be left without any access to education at all.

My purpose is not to make a detailed argument for the involvement of state and federal government in providing basic education for children. The point here is that the market, on its own, especially in a highly competitive consumerist economy, cannot provide this basic need with any equity. The education of children is not best described as a commodity. This leads us to bring a critical eye to another intersection of commercialized culture and education: the much touted public/private partnerships.

Sharon Beder comments on the motivation behind corporate partnerships with public education from the perspective of the private sector partners: "Corporations preferred to give small amounts of money through gifts and sponsorships and be seen as benefactors, than to pay the taxes required to fully fund the schools."[63] Alex Molnar notes that what corporations donate to educational efforts is a mere fraction of the tax relief that they receive after extensive lobbying efforts.[64] He writes,

> The ability of local tax payers to raise and spend money for education determines to a large extent the quality of the educational opportunities that children receive. Rather than address this self-evident truth, it's become very popular to say that the problem is that poor districts aren't spending money efficiently. The difficulty with that for the people who advance the argument—although it's very obviously appealing politically and it certainly plays well to corporate executives—is that if you look at the amount of administrative overhead in the public sector, you see that the public schools are, in fact, much leaner and much more efficient than the private sector.[65]

According to Molnar, "the language of corporate school reform is the language of 'human resources' and 'human capital.'"[66] Of a 1992 United States Labor Department report entitled "Learning for Living" Molnar writes,

> Despite its advocacy of some sound teaching principles, the report gave no consideration to the aspirations and dreams of children. In fact, a person searching through corporate reform literature would, in general, have little hope of finding concern about educational equity for girls or minority group members or about the simple justice of spending at least the same amount of money to educate

each child. Nor do corporate-sponsored reforms consider the possibility that perhaps we should provide decent, humane schools for all our children because we love them and because childhood in the United States should be a rich and rewarding time during which children learn to care for each other through the example of adults who care for them.[67]

Children are not considered in their own right and many of their needs are not addressed in any meaningful way through these reforms. Education ultimately serves the profit incentive of corporate America instead of serving children. There is no doubt that children should be educated for participation in public life; in the best circumstances that includes but is not limited to participation through work for which they must be prepared. This is only one element of the education that is demanded by the human personhood of children, the fullness of which cannot be measured through standardized testing and purely vocational training.

Molnar is quite clear about the limits of the market in providing education for children:

> Education is a public good. We all suffer or we all benefit if education is well provided. We all suffer or we all benefit if children are treated fairly and taught well. A market, by definition, can't address issues of equity. Nor, do I think a market can provide public education and make a profit as long as equity concerns are a factor in the equation.[68]

Molnar researches the involvement of for-profit (both privately and publicly held) corporations in providing education through charter schools and contracts with public school systems. Edison and Beacon are two such corporations who claim to be able to provide a quality education that improves student performance all while making a profit. The profit is made not through success in its educational efforts but rather by going public, through the trading of stock. We should pause to reflect on the implications of having the education of poor students be a commodity that is bought and sold on the open market with only the profit incentive to guide it.

Stock in corporations like Edison Schools has fluctuated. When there is money to be made, investors hold on and then sell out when the stock begins to dip. This does not represent a commitment to children in "failing" schools. Publicly held for-profit education corporations are accountable to the shareholders and not to children and their families. They are accountable to the public only in the sense that a contract might not be renewed if student performance does not improve to the satisfaction of the public sector. According to its website, Edison is currently operating in 157 public schools in the United States (mainly through charter schools). Their advertising portrays

Edison as a partner in the project of public education, but unlike the government, they are not required to remain in this endeavor when it ceases to be profitable for their shareholders.[69]

Jonathan Kozol, a longtime friend to the poorest children in New York City, has claimed that the United States, the wealthiest country in the world, tolerates apartheid in its public school systems.[70] Many poor children, often children of color, are denied access to an adequate education. Systematic injustices, fueled by racism and classism (and perhaps sexism), perpetuate this two-tiered approach to education. According to Kozol, "there are few areas in which the value we attribute to a child's life may be so clearly measured as in the decisions that we make about the money we believe it's worth investing in the education of one person's child as opposed to that of someone else's child."[71]

In his books, Kozol has given readers haunting pictures of what it means to be a poor child in the United States.[72] He exposes the failures on the part of communities, governments, health care institutions and schools to enhance the well-being of children. His portraits of the children themselves are not romanticized, but their voices are insightful and provocative. Once again, the blame for the situation that poor children in the inner cities of the United States find themselves cannot be laid at one door. Yet, Kozol's experience intersects with our discussion of commercialism and children in several important ways. The first and most obvious is recognized by Schor: "The main impetus for commercialization [in education] is the chronic underfunding of schools."[73] Susan Linn agrees:

> Those in the education trenches who allow, if not embrace, corporate marketing in their schools—superintendents, principles, teachers, and school board members—don't justify it on philosophical, political, or educational grounds, nor do they suggest that it is in the best interest of children to use school as a marketplace. For them, it comes down to money.[74]

Linn argues that the "commercialization of childhood" received impetus in the 1980s during the Reagan administration. Advertising was largely deregulated, allowing programming for children with deliberate advertising intent; that is to say it allowed the creation of shows for the express purpose of selling toys. This combined with drastically reduced federal funding for public institutions including public schools to create an overly commercialized atmosphere for children. She claims that schools in particular were encouraged to seek help, in the form of funding, from corporate America.[75]

Again we have an issue that could be considered from any number of angles. We will approach this reflection on education in the United States by focusing on the "savage inequalities" that exist between the rich and poor in the public school systems illustrated by Jonathan Kozol.[76] As public policy makers determine the resources available for public education, the poorest children suffer. Poor children continue to have fewer resources, and this has consequences for the ways in which their present and future participation in public life takes shape. As with many issues confronting the world's children, adequate education for all children will only be achieved through the participation of many spheres of civil society, including the public and private sectors.

There are many programs that seek greater involvement on the part of corporate America in providing education. These public-private partnerships may seem promising, yet they may also reveal the potential dangers of relying on a market-based approach to providing this basic need. These partnerships often involve providing equipment and resources to desperate schools in exchange for marketing access to the children. Other programs emphasize the production of skilled workers for the U.S. economy even in the face of staggering unemployment.

The expansion of market logic into education is not new and is not limited to the direct incursion of advertising or corporate partnerships. In her research on the history of school education, Sharon Beder notes that there has always been a tension between two distinct visions of the ends of education. On the one hand, education has been undertaken with a view toward very practical goals that include producing dutiful workers and instilling "economically desirable values and behavior." On the other hand, education has been thought of as good in itself, irrespective of its practical applications, and "should develop the human potential of individual children without reference to what might be expected of them as workers in the future."[77] Kozol's observations suggest that educators have limited goals with respect to poor children: keeping them contained or training them to be dutiful workers in factories or service industries. Children of privilege on the other hand, are encouraged to be creative, and to strive for leadership in the professions. Beder notes, "Whilst work-based learning in schools and universities has obvious benefits for employers, the benefits to students themselves and the society are more ambiguous. A major difference between training and education is that training is aimed at shaping a person toward a specific end, whereas education is aimed at giving people choices in life."[78] Purely vocational education cannot give young people a sense of the meaning of work in our lives and communities or even a critical understanding of the rights of workers. Adult obsession with work, which Beder claims is fueled by rampant consumerism in the United States, is passed on to children, giving market logic free rein even in our schools.

Beder goes on to note, "There is an increasing trend for middle-class American children to be sent to some organized activity after school rather than coming home to play freely in the neighborhood. Such activities, including sporting activities, are often competitive, particularly as the children get older and more involved, and incorporate 'performance criteria' into their play."[79] She is concerned here with extension of "performance" and other corporate and competitive models into the lives of young children who, it is assumed, should be free for imaginative play and learning. Again, we are reminded of the hurried, over-programmed child, who is not allowed to enjoy childhood, but is rather pressured to compete and achieve success. It is important to note that Beder is referring here to middle class (and perhaps upper-middle class and wealthy children). Somewhat mirroring concerns about work, we hear lamenting about what all of this involvement is doing to children, while those who are advocating on behalf of poor children are calling for increased commitment to after-school programs as a key component to violence prevention initiatives.[80] Many of their neighborhoods are unfortunately unsafe for playing freely.

Poor children who need activities to keep them safe, healthy, and growing in self-esteem do not have the resources to access them. Wealthy children, who have access to numerous activities, may be inordinately directed toward those that encourage competitive behavior. Both of these situations seem unacceptable. Given the prevalence of two-wage-earner households (and households in which the only parent works), all children should have access to after-school programming. A Christian ethical perspective would certainly see value in sporting activities but would also balance these with service-oriented activities. That is to say that a sense of teamwork, success, and self-worth can be found not only by competing with and defeating an opposing team, but also by serving others (for example, neighborhood cleanup, staffing a Special Olympics tournament, or a day spent with Habitat for Humanity).

The market child is clearly in view. Children, especially poor children in our public schools, are viewed with these images in mind: the child as burden; the child as producer and as future dutiful worker; the child who is open to the manipulations of marketing strategies and who can be easily encouraged to consume; and the child who through the buying and selling of stock is herself essentially a commodity. Even privileged children are vulnerable to the negative effects of this extension of market metaphors. While their basic needs are more than being met, they are also often encouraged to consume without contributing and to demonstrate a competitive edge favored by the market even in their play.

The signs of the times for many of the world's children are troubling to say the least. The claims we make about our commitment to children as gifts from God and our hope for a better future are exposed as rhetorical flourish that often fails to find concrete expression in market practices. Children in the carpet factories, agricultural fields, and red-light districts need more than our rhetoric. Child poverty, exploitative child labor, and advertising to children are complex issues that meet with no simple solutions; but to give up in the face of such complexity is to abdicate our responsibilities. Having a sense of the narratives and the numbers that make up the stories of childhood today, we look to traditions that can assist in moving us forward. Two different and often conflicting ethical frameworks emerge in response to these concerns, children's rights and family values, each with distinctive approaches and concrete strategies for building a "world fit for children."

Notes

1. Danna Nolan Fewell, *The Children of Israel: Reading the Bible for the Sake of Our Children* (Nashville, TN: Abingdon Press, 2003), 69.

2. Craig Kielburger with Kevin Major, *Free the Children: A Young Man Fights Against Child Labor and Proves That Children Can Change the World* (New York: Harper Perennial, 2000).

3. The details of Iqbal's life and death are not entirely clear and there remains controversy about elements of his story, including his age, the reasons for his stunted growth (which no doubt had been exacerbated if not entirely caused by his work in the factory), and the circumstances surrounding his death. This confusion contributes to worries that children can be manipulated and exploited even by those who purport to advocate for them. Children have, as Hugh Cunningham has noted, "immense propaganda potential." Craig Kielburger wrestles with conflicting accounts of Iqbal's life and the impact this has on his work for children in *Free the Children*.

4. Tanya Roberts-Davis, *We Need to Go to School: Voices of the RugMark Children* (Toronto: Groundwood, 2001), 4. RugMark strives to eliminate the exploitation of children in the carpet industry by providing educational opportunities as well as certifying rugs made without the use of child labor. See www.rugmark.org (accessed May 11, 2009).

5. Kielburger, *Free the Children*, 290–91.

6. *Gaudium et Spes* (*The Church in the Modern World*, 1965), 1. The document is available at www.vatican.va/archive/hist_councils/ii_vatican_council/documents/vat-ii_const_19651207_gaudium-et-spes_en.html (accessed May 16, 2009).

7. United Nations Special Session on Children, New York, 2002, www.un.org/ga/children/ (accessed January 4, 2009).

8. United States Conference of Catholic Bishops, "Charter for the Protection of Children and Youth," www.usccb.org/ocyp/charter.pdf (accessed May 5, 2009).

9. Children's Defense Fund, www.childrensdefense.org. Statistics are from August 2004. (June 2005).

10. Children's Defense Fund, www.childrensdefense.org/data/america.aspx.

11. Children's Defense Fund information can be found at www.childrensdefense .org. Statistics on children's poverty are a moving target, no doubt impacted by the crisis in the global financial markets in 2008–2009. The CDF monitors developments in the U.S. budgetary process (May 6, 2009).

12. Children's Defense Fund, www.childrensdefense.org/data/keyfacts.aspx.

13. The United States Census Bureau data from 2007 indicates that although poverty rates for people in the eighteen to sixty-four and sixty-five and older age categories was statistically unchanged between 2006 and 2007, "both the poverty rate and the number in poverty increased for children under 18 years old (18.0 percent and 13.3 million in 2007, up from 17.4 percent and 12.8 million in 2006). The poverty rate for children was higher than the rates for people 18 to 64 years old and those 65 and older. Children represented 35.7 percent of the people in poverty and 24.8 percent of the total population." Carmen DeNavas-Walt, Bernadette D. Proctor, and Jessica C. Smith, *Income, Poverty, and Health Insurance Coverage in the United States: 2007* (Washington, DC: U.S. Government Printing Office, 2008), 60–235. For the CDF press release responding to Census Bureau data see www.childrensdefense.org/site/PageServer?pagename=newsroom_20080826_CensusData (accessed September 17, 2008).

14. UNICEF, *Official Summary: The State of the World's Children, 2004*, 3, www .unicef.org/publications/files/2004_OfficialSumm_ENG.pdf.

15. UNICEF, "Facts on Children," www.unicef.org/media/media_fastfacts.html.

16. UNICEF, www.unicef.org/media/media_9479.html and www.unicef.org/media/media_9745.html.

17. Donald H. Dunson, *Child, Victim, Soldier: The Loss of Innocence in Uganda* (Maryknoll, NY: Orbis, 2008), 18.

18. Dunson, *Child, Victim, Soldier*, 18.

19. Donald H. Dunson, *No Room at the Table: Earth's Most Vulnerable Children* (Maryknoll, NY: Orbis, 2003).

20. Dunson, *Child, Victim, Soldier*, 8.

21. Paul Farmer, *Pathologies of Power: Health, Human Rights and the New War on the Poor* (Berkeley: University of California Press, 2003). Mary J. McDonough, *Can a Health Care Market Be Moral? A Catholic Vision* (Washington, DC: Georgetown University Press, 2007).

22. Jim McKechnie and Sandy Hobbs, "Child Labour: The View from the North," *Childhood* 6, no. 1 (1999): 89–90.

23. Hugh D. Hindman, *Child Labor: An American History* (Armonk, NY: M. E. Sharpe, 2002), 294.

24. Hindman, *Child Labor*, 293.

25. Hindman, *Child Labor*, 294.

26. Hindman, *Child Labor*, 295.

27. Agnes Zenaida V. Camacho, "Family, Child Labour and Migration: Child Domestic workers in Metro Manila," *Children* 6, no. 1 (1999): 57–73.

28. Julia O'Connell Davidson, *Children in the Global Sex Trade* (Cambridge: Polity Press, 2005).

29. Hindman, *Child Labor*, 297.

30. Robert D. Putnam, *Bowling Alone: The Collapse and Revival of American Community* (New York: Simon and Schuster, 2000).

31. Kiku Adatto, "Selling Out Childhood," *The Hedgehog Review* 5, no. 2 (Summer 2003): 24–40.

32. The International Labour Organization adopted Convention No. 182 on "The Worst Forms of Child Labour" in 1999. Rather than focusing on the elimination of all labor of children under the age of eighteen, this convention focuses on forms of labor including sex work and trafficking. This becomes problematic for children's organizations, which define these as crimes and not legitimate forms of work.

33. Juliet B. Schor, "America's Most Wanted," *Boston College Magazine*, 64, no. 4 (Fall 2004): 30–37.

34. Schor, "America's Most Wanted," 30.

35. Schor, "America's Most Wanted," 31.

36. A recent *Globe Magazine* cover story discussed the impact of violent media, especially video gaming, on children and adults. While most of the concern is often on whether exposure to these games (because unlike television and movies they are interactive with first person killing) increases violent behavior, the article raises other issues related to our present discussion. Rather than encouraging violent behavior itself, these games may be more effective at instilling an attitude of passivity or desensitizing in the face of real conflict or violence. Gamers may develop technical skills needed for a technology-based economy, but they may also become docile employees whose work life and leisure time bear a very close resemblance. Tracy Mayor, "What Are Video Games Turning Us Into?" *Boston Globe Magazine*, February 20, 2005, 18–21, 32–37.

37. Susan Linn, *Consuming Kids: The Hostile Takeover of Childhood* (New York: The New Press, 2004), 11–30. Schor also makes note of the language of ad campaigns highlighting its use of combat metaphors like "target," "collateral," and "viral marketing." Schor, "America's Most Wanted," 30.

38. Juliet B. Schor, *Born to Buy: The Commercialized Child and the New Consumer Culture* (New York: Scribner, 2004), 114–17.

39. Juliet B. Schor, "The Commodification of Childhood: Tales from the Advertising Front Lines," *The Hedgehog Review* 5, no. 2 (Spring 2003): 7–23.

40. Linn, *Consuming Kids*, 36.

41. Schor, *Born to Buy*, 115.

42. Schor, *Born to Buy*, 108.

43. Schor, *Born to Buy*, 108.

44. Juliet B. Schor, "Appendix C: Commercial Alert's Parents' Bill of Rights," in *Born to Buy*, 217–19 at 217.

45. Tim Coffey, David Siegel, and Greg Livingston, *Mom and Kid: Marketing to the New Super Consumer* (Ithaca, NY: Paramount Market Publishing, 2006), ix.

46. Coffey, *Mom and Kid*, 6.

47. Coffey, *Mom and Kid*, x.

48. Coffey, *Mom and Kid*, 185.

49. David Walsh, *Selling Out America's Children: How America Puts Profits before Values and What Parents Can Do* (Minneapolis: Fairview Press, 1994).

50. Coffey, *Mom and Kid*, x. See also David Walsh, *Selling Out America's Children*, ix.

51. Linn, *Consuming Kids*, 1.

52. Diane Ravitch and Joseph P. Viteritti, eds., *Kid Stuff: Marketing Sex and Violence to America's Children* (Baltimore: Johns Hopkins University Press, 2003), 5.

53. Kay S. Hymowitz, "The Contradictions of Parenting in a Media Age," in *Kid Stuff: Marketing Sex and Violence to America's Children*, ed. Diane Ravitch and Joseph P. Viteritti (Baltimore: Johns Hopkins University Press, 2003), 214–39 at 217. Citing: Bradley Greenberg, Philip M. Erikson, and Mantha Vlahos, "Children's Television Viewing Behavior as Perceived by Mother and Child," in *Television and Social Behavior*, vol. 4, ed. E. A. Rubinstein, George Comstock, and J. P. Murray (Washington, DC: U.S. Government Printing Office, 1972).

54. Schor, *Born to Buy*, 141–75. The relationship between advertising, consumer culture and these detrimental outcomes is complex. Which comes first, the depression or the high exposure to consumer culture? Her research suggests that children who suffer from depression are not more likely to seek out access to consumer culture, suggesting that the relationship does indeed move in the opposite direction. Nevertheless, debate will continue about the relationships of causality and correlation. Schor, *Born to Buy*, 166–67.

55. Linn, *Consuming Kids*, 1.

56. Walsh, *Selling Out America's Children*, 142–43.

57. Researchers at Michigan State University have outlined the effects of advertising on children and divided these into two categories: intended and unintended effects. They list brand recognition, product desires, product purchase requests, consumption patterns and persuasive appeals among the intended effects of advertising. They include parent-child conflict, unhappiness, unhealthy eating habits, materialism, and negative self-perception among the unintended effects of advertising to children. Stacy L. Smith and Charles Atkin, "Television Advertising and Children: Examining the Intended and Unintended Effects," in *The Faces of Televisual Media: Teaching, Violence, Selling to Children*, ed. Edward L. Palmer and Brian M. Young (Mahwah, NJ: Lawrence Eerlbaum Associates, 2003), 301–25 at 306–17. Critics like Schor and Linn would be quick to point out that since many of these effects have been documented in the research, it becomes disingenuous to claim they are "unintended." These effects are foreseen and to a certain extent directly intended. For example, advertising aims at creating dissatisfaction and unhappiness with one's present possessions and patterns of consumption. The whole point is to desire something else, something new. Moreover, ads claim that happiness can be achieved through material possessions and patterns of consumption. It is simply not the case that advertising merely tolerates these negative side effects as the price to be paid for flourishing industry. Much of the advertising strategies discussed here are based on these "unintended consequences" as their premises.

58. Michael J. McGinnis, Jennifer Grootman, and Vivica I. Kraak, *Food Marketing to Children and Youth: Threat or Opportunity?* (Washington, DC: National Academies Press, 2006), xiv.

59. McGinnis, *Food Marketing*, 1.

60. James U. McNeal, *The Kids Market: Myths and Realities* (Ithaca, NY: Paramount Market Publishing, 1999), 247.

61. Schor, *Born to Buy*, 85.

62. Jeff Jacoby, "Separating School and State" *Boston Globe*, June 12, 2005, D11.

63. Sharon Beder, *Selling the Work Ethic: From Puritan Pulpit to Corporate PR* (London and New York: Zed Books, 2000), 201.

64. Molnar claims that in 1989 corporate giving to public elementary schools totaled $156 million. Donations to private schools and colleges and universities totaled $2.4 billion. Corporations in Wisconsin alone received more the $1 billion in tax breaks. Alex Molnar, *Giving Kids the Business: The Commercialization of America's Schools* (Boulder, CO: Westview Press, 1996), 8.

65. Information on Molnar's research was initially found at the Education Policy Studies Laboratory/Commercialism in Education Research Institute at Arizona State University. The site is currently located at the Education and the Public Interest Research Center/Commercialism in Education Research Unit at the School of Education of the University of Colorado at Boulder, at epicpolicy.org/ceru-home (accessed May 16, 2009).

66. Molnar, *Giving Kids the Business*, 4.

67. Molnar, *Giving Kids the Business*, 4–5.

68. Molnar, *Giving Kids the Business*.

69. Information on Edison, its mission, board, schools, and advertising campaigns can be found at www.edisonlearning.com (accessed January 4, 2009).

70. Jonathan Kozol, *Savage Inequalities: Children in America's Schools* (New York: Harper Perennial, 1992).

71. Jonathan Kozol, *Ordinary Resurrections: Children in the Years of Hope* (New York: Crown Publishers, 2000), 44.

72. Kozol's other works include *Rachel and Her Children: Homeless Families in America* (New York: Fawcett Columbine, 1989) and *Amazing Grace: The Lives of Children and the Conscience of a Nation* (New York: Perennial, 2000).

73. Schor, *Born to Buy*, 90.

74. Linn, *Consuming Kids*, 78.

75. Linn, *Consuming Kids*, 6–7.

76. Kozol, *Savage Inequalities*.

77. Beder, *Selling the Work Ethic*, 195–96.

78. Beder, *Selling the Work Ethic*, 218.

79. Beder, *Selling the Work Ethic*, 198.

80. See www.childrensdefense.org/site/PageNavigator/policy_ecd_after_school (accessed January 4, 2009).

2

Children's Rights and Family Values

CONSUMER CULTURE IS PLAYING an increasing role in the lives of children, shaping many forms of their participation in the life of the community. Among the privileged, children are consumers, being educated to spend their family resources to their own individual benefit. Advertising is viewed as a tool for this education, expanding children's awareness of the range of choices and propelling the never ending expansion of those choices. Education itself has become a commodity, sought after not only to secure flourishing but also to gain advantage. Among poor children, the most devastating form of economic participation is exploitative labor in all its forms: factory wage labor, sex work, soldiering, domestic labor, and agriculture. These children are themselves consumed; their exploitation is widespread and yet remains hidden in the shadows.

Both ends of this spectrum take a toll on children's bodies, spirits, and relationships and are in need of redress with poor children having the most urgent claim to our committed action. How should we craft public policy that fosters the well-being of children? Do children need protection, and if so, from whom and from what? Do children need liberation? *From* whom or what do they need to be liberated? *For* what do they need to be liberated? Which children are considered vulnerable and in need of protection? Which children are thought of as "trouble makers," threats to the public order, in need of discipline and character-building work?

Approaches to current public policies effecting children in this context generally fall into two main categories, each of which have found allies in Christian communities.[1] Following the movement for universal human rights, many advocates for children's well-being argue from a rights-based approach and demand compliance with the United Nations' 1989 document, the *Convention on the Rights of the Child* (*CRC*). Others approach the challenges facing children by focusing on the family: successful families mean successful and thriving children. While it is hard to argue against the proposition that children flourish in loving families who have access to important resources, this focus on family-based advantages often appears to encourage traditional, patriarchal family structures at the expense of families that do not fit the mold.

Each of these models is, in its own way, an answer to a third approach outlined in the previous chapter: the market will take care of children. Grounded in confidence in the free market economy, this approach maintains that the market, left to its own devices of supply and demand and profit incentives, will do the best job of distributing the goods and services that children need to grow. Many social ethicists recognize that the influence of market forces on our common life together ought to be subjected to a great deal of scrutiny, and so this attention to the overall economy is a critical piece of any approach to policy that impacts the lives of children. Critics point out that an unfettered free market economy has extended itself into other areas of life in ways that often work against the recognition of human dignity. Children are encouraged to be avid consumers, and have themselves become objects of exchange in the market. The often noted examples are the burgeoning fertility industry and some private adoption practices. Hidden from view are the millions of children who are serving the market through their labor. Children who do not participate in the market either as laborers or consumers are considered merely as financial burdens on families and society at large. Our reading of the signs of the times for children has clearly illustrated the dangers present when we give priority to the market.

As we have seen, criticizing the influence that consumer market culture has on our children has become par for the course among parents and those promoting the well-being of children, though the nature of the criticisms and proposed remedies vary. What follows is a closer examination of the children's rights and family values approaches as they shape public debate about the well-being of children. They also have points of convergence with the market-based approach. Even as they react to the influence of market culture, rights supporters and family advocates often accept many free market assumptions. An adequate Christian perspective on children will incorporate elements of both perspectives; keeping them in creative tension with each other may serve to lessen the liabilities they face when each approach operates on its own. The vision of children and the common good that will be proposed in chapter 3 will draw on the distinctive strengths of the rights-based, family-centered perspectives, folding them into an outlook grounded in the anthropological commitments of Catholic social teaching.

The Movement for Children's Rights

One very prominent organization in the United States advocating on behalf of children is the Children's Defense Fund (CDF), founded by Marian Wright Edelman, who as of this writing remains its director and most powerful spokesperson. As we saw in chapter 1, the CDF researches and publishes information on the well-being of children in its *Yearbook.* The mission statement of the Children's Defense Fund makes a claim about what children "deserve" as children, as human beings. While the language does not use the term "rights" the rationale behind the statement is consistent with this approach. The mission of the CDF reads,

> The mission of the Children's Defense Fund is to *Leave No Child Behind* and to ensure every child. . . . A Healthy Start, A Head Start, A Fair Start, A Safe Start, A Moral Start, in life and a successful passage to adulthood with the help of caring families and communities.[2]

The healthy, head, fair, safe and moral "starts" that the CDF seeks are directly related to children's needs and the legitimate claims they can make on the community. Children deserve adequate nutrition, access to quality education (even in the preschool years), safe neighborhoods, and opportunities to grow in the moral life. The demands that the CDF makes on behalf of children, especially poor children, directly impinge on how adults envision their responsibilities and relationships. The CDF challenges adults to transform their lives and to act in the best interests of children who suffer both from material poverty and what Pamela Couture calls the "poverty of tenuous connections."[3]

The Children's Defense Fund is just one example of an organization driven to ensure children's human rights, and along with other organizations, like UNICEF, for example, its mission is in many ways an attempt to live out the mandates of the *Convention on the Rights of the Child*, which forms the cornerstone of contemporary debates about children's rights. The *Convention* frequently serves as the benchmark for assessing the well-being of children around the world. Before looking at this document and its implications in greater detail, we will first consider briefly the emergence of the movement for children's rights in which we can place contemporary organizations like the CDF or UNICEF. This history is important for our present task because we must be alert to the assumptions about childhood that have been operative in the movement in order to see how these continue to shape our attempts to secure child well-being.

Historian Hugh Cunningham has detailed the emergence of philanthropic and state movements for the protection of children in Great Britain.[4] The Industrial Revolution, bringing with it the ability for mass production, often involved the movement of people from the countryside where an agrarian society had once thrived, to the cities as they sought work in the factories. The need for families to provide for themselves combined with the need for more inexpensive labor created a space for child wage labor in the industrial sector. Now as we have seen, children in previous centuries were not strangers to work. They had often worked on family farms, in cottage industries, as the caretakers of younger siblings, and as apprentices to skilled laborers. That children worked was nothing new. That children could be exploited for their labor (on farms, in domestic service, as slaves and sex workers) was also nothing new. What was different were their working conditions and the ease with which large numbers of children could be exploited to increase profits. This form of work and the potential for exploitation was more visible in the new institution of the factory. Added to the changing perceptions about children and childhood, this situation sparked increased concern and critique on the part of philanthropists and others concerned about the changes wrought by industrialization.

Similarly, the United States saw the emergence of Children's Aid Societies in the nineteenth century. The image of the family as an organic unit in which each member had a place that entailed mutual rights and responsibilities was still prevalent. Such a model of family, and children's place therein, could not according to historian Joseph Hawes, "address the problem of children who seemed to be living by their wits on city streets in the middle of the nineteenth century." We must not be too sanguine about the motivations of the aid societies in rescuing children; they "sprang up basically to rid the streets of these disturbing reminders that the expansion of the American economy and the American city had taken a terrible toll on the families of the lower orders."[5] The aid of poor children often went hand in hand with a moral judgment passed on their parents' inability to meet the demands of an ideal family, in which children are seen and not heard, silent until spoken too. Children in burgeoning urban centers seemed to live by social rules all their own.

The emergence of the public or common school was often the cornerstone of public policy with respect to children and went hand in hand with debates about the nature of children's work. Hawes notes the influence of *parens patriae* or the notion that the state is the parent of all children.[6] Such ultimate responsibility could justify both compulsory education for children on the one hand, and arguments advocating for work on behalf of poorer children on the other. Both of these would cultivate civic responsibility and promote social values.

Another claim to parentage would be exercised in a sense by the Catholic Church in the United States. Efforts were underway at the turn of the twentieth century to abolish child labor by means of a constitutional amendment. Labor unions, seeking to protect adult employment, and aid societies both supported the measure. It was opposed by farmers, factory owners, and the church, most notably in the person of William Cardinal O'Connell, the archbishop of Boston. The claim was that such a measure "would ultimately lead to the usurpation of parental rights in education" and the demise of parochial schooling. The latter, it cannot be denied was a crucial medium for ecclesiastical control of the young—the church in the form of the clergy, being the father of all children as it were.[7]

Though children have not figured prominently in the documentary heritage of Catholic social teaching, a concern for their well-being in the world of work is voiced in Pope Leo XIII's 1891 encyclical *Rerum Novarum*, a document that bears the English title *The Condition of Labor*. Leo XIII wrote,

> And in regard to children, great care should be taken not to place them in workshops and factories until their bodies and minds are sufficiently mature. For just as rough weather destroys the buds of spring, so too early an experience of life's hard work blights the young promise of a child's powers, and makes any real education impossible.[8]

Though it appeared as a minor point in the encyclical, the pope did express concern for the vulnerability of young minds and bodies that should preclude certain types of labor. It is not necessarily child labor itself that is prohibited, but rather work that is exploitative or harsh for young and immature bodies. He wrote that "work which is suitable for a strong man cannot reasonably be required from a woman or a child."[9] The encyclical also maintained an organic vision of the family, one more at home in an agrarian society. This leaves room for children's work in the home or on the farm, but potentially without adequate concern for the ways in which this too could be exploitative or damaging to children's potential. The overall concern seems to stem from a sense that early exposure to the world of work in industrializing societies, that is work apart from the family, will hinder attempts at education, and perhaps reduce the sphere of influence from parents and the church. While the document does not address the situation of working children in any sustained way, *Rerum Novarum* does begin a tradition of teachings that engage economic matters and the dignity of human work. It inaugurates what will become the documentary heritage of Catholic social teaching which grounds the common good perspective on children and childhood articulated in chapter 3.

Remarkably, decades later concern for the well-being of children was compelling enough that Pope Benedict XV encouraged Catholics to support the work of Save the Children. Founded in the early twentieth century by Eglantyne Jebb, a Protestant activist, as a response to the devastation of World War I, Save the Children sought to ease the suffering of children in Europe who were the innocent victims of war and the enmity between the victors and the vanquished. Pope Benedict XV published several documents addressing the situation of children in Central Europe and in these he encouraged Catholics to support relief efforts. What is remarkable is that the documents specifically mention Save the Children. Funds collected in parishes and dioceses were to be given, if not to the Holy See, then to Save the Children. According to Margaret Eletta Guider, Pope Benedict XV did not give way to the "predictable judgments of ecclesiastical zealots known for their acerbic criticisms of potentially compromising alliances. Contrary to the logic of polity, however, he embraced the logic of the gospel."[10] Even longstanding ecumenical disputes could not come between those who sought to relieve the suffering of poor children. Those in power are called on to move beyond politics and ecumenical divisions for the sake of children.

Movements that sought to secure better conditions for children in the aftermath of World War I and amidst the growing influence of industrialization had wide appeal. Ms. Jebb appeared before the League of Nations to present a *Declaration on the Rights of the Child* some twenty-five years before the *Universal Declaration on Human Rights* in 1948.[11] The *Declaration* was adopted by the League of Nations in 1924.[12] A more recent incarnation of the *Declaration* is the United Nations *Convention on the Rights of the Child* (*CRC*), adopted by the General Assembly in November of 1989. It was ratified by an overwhelming majority of member nations with the notable exceptions of the United States and Somalia.[13] In May of 2002, the United Nations hosted a Special Session on Children in order to evaluate progress toward fulfilling the mandates of the *Convention on the Rights of the Child*.[14] The *Convention* has enjoyed widespread support even though conflicts over parental rights and reproductive freedoms for young people have continued to spark debate. The 2002 Special Session was able to rejoice in the advances that have been made in the last ten years even as it had to face the many remaining obstacles to children's well-being.[15]

The UN *Convention on the Rights of the Child* provides a comprehensive list of children's rights, which are in effect adult responsibilities toward children and young people. Like human rights more broadly considered, children's rights are both economic and political. Children have rights to adequate food, shelter, clothing, education, and health care. They have a right to be free from exploitation, trafficking, and any other labor that may threaten their health and development. Children also have a right to a name and a nationality as well as the right to participate in their culture, especially when they are also members of minority or indigenous populations. Moreover, children and young people have the right to rest and recreation appropriate to their age.

More controversial for some are children's rights to freedom of expression, thought, conscience, religion, association, and privacy. These are claims that the children of the world can make on their parents and families, the wider community, governments, and churches. The possibility that asserting these rights may bring children and youth into conflict with adults is very real. The control that parents and families have over children is limited. Problematic here is the tacit assumption that children have the capacity to consistently recognize what is in their own best interest. Many parents would be quick to note that children and young people sometimes desire things that could be harmful, and are therefore vulnerable to exploitation or manipulation by other adults. Nevertheless, the *CRC* raises the critical claim that parental and familial power and control over children cannot be absolute, and their influence must narrow as children mature. Children's rights are subject to restriction only in so far as the exercise of those rights may threaten the child herself, the public order, or the well-being of others. Decisions made on behalf of children must have the best interests of the child as the standard criterion, though how to distill a child's best interest amidst the legitimate interests of others is at best a complicated task.

These criteria stem from the UN's conviction that "the child should be fully prepared to live an individual life in society, and brought up in the spirit of ideals proclaimed in the Charter of the United Nations, and in particular in the spirit of peace, dignity, tolerance, freedom, equality and solidarity."[16] The comprehensive, though not perhaps exhaustive, list of rights detailed in the *CRC* form what the United Nations considers to be the *minimum* conditions that children require to thrive. Wherever the law may provide higher standards, then the higher standards would necessarily prevail.[17]

Questions emerge as to whether or not the *CRC* imagines an autonomous and independent child and fails to take seriously children's real vulnerability and dependence on adults, who in general do act to safeguard the well-being of children as they mature. This suspicion about the wisdom of enacting a charter of rights for children seems to stem from a concern about the rights of parents to direct the lives of their children and a desire to protect the autonomy of the family unit.[18] The notion of children's rights is also in many ways in tension with the image of childhood innocence. Hugh Cunningham remarks, "The peculiarity of the late twentieth century, and the root cause of much present confusion and angst about childhood, is that a public discourse which argues that children are persons with rights to a degree of autonomy is at odds with the remnants of the romantic view that the right of a child is to be a child."[19]

In a searing critique of the *CRC*, considering it tantamount to child abandonment, Bruce C. Hafen and Jonathan O. Hafen claim that this unprecedented emphasis on children's autonomy is more concerned with children's free choices than with their protection.[20] According to the Hafens, children, from the perspective of the *CRC*, are identical to adults. This suggestion in the *CRC* does not arise from any evidence that children possess "adult-like capacity" but rather from what the Hafens term "the liberationist ideology that kids are people too."[21]

Martin Guggenheim also joins the critics of the children's rights movement, but he makes the distinction between two sets of rights in his critique: "the rights of children with respect to the exercise of state power; and the other, the rights of children with respect to the exercise of parental authority." In regard to the area of family relationships, governed by parental authority, Guggenheim says, "I am far less confident that children need rights or that speaking in terms of 'rights' is even good for children."[22] This emphasis on parental claims to authority over their children leads Guggenheim in a direction not articulated by the Hafens:

> Children are inherently dependent for much of the time they remain in the category of "child." For this reason, it is highly problematic to discuss the rights of children in a wide variety of contexts without simultaneously considering the rights of the people on whom they are dependent. In our culture, this means their parents. Attempting to consider the rights and needs of (very young) children without simultaneously taking into account the rights and needs of their parents is akin to attempting to isolate someone's arm from the rest of their body.[23]

Like the family-centered approach to be discussed shortly, Guggenheim's argument refuses to pit children's interests against that of their family and views the family, principally the parents, as the route through which claims against society and the state are exercised. His insistence on recognizing the dependence of children on adults who have charge of their care is a crucial element of an adequate view of children's rights, as is the claim that children's well-being depends in large measure on their parents ability to exercise fundamental rights both economic and political. But we must also recognize that children are *not* an appendage of the family, as an arm to a body.

A Christian perspective on children and childhood cannot reduce the "kids are people too" argument to mere ideology. Children's fundamental human dignity, the concept that the phrase, "kids are people too," attempts to capture, cannot be dismissed so easily by anyone who claims to have children's best interests at heart. Their dignity is no different and no less than that of any adult. Child development psychologist Penelope Leach, arguing from a secular perspective, makes a similar claim: "Human rights must include children because they are human. . . . That phrase, 'children's rights,' is only needed because children have been excluded."[24] Elsewhere she writes, "No society can claim to do its best for children as children unless what it does is based on acceptance of children as people."[25] Children are not merely our creations, possessions, or objects of adult concern, "they are us."[26]

Nevertheless, some of the Hafens' concerns need to be addressed, particularly the concern that an increase in children's freedoms may "reflect a lessening of adult responsibility for children" and may fail to consider the burdens that come with such freedoms.[27] They write,

> But some adults who want to liberate children are not as motivated by children's interests as by their own interests—some ideological and some that merely serve adult convenience. Adults face a conflict of interest in thinking about autonomy for children. When they disengage themselves from the arduous task of rearing and teaching children in the name of increasing children's autonomy, adults' actual—even if not fully conscious—purpose may be to increase their own autonomy by freeing themselves from the burdens of providing meaningful care. Even worse, some pro-child autonomy claims are merely a smokescreen intended to protect the interests of adults who profit from such claims while indirectly exploiting the actual interests of children. . . . The assertion that untutored, unguided children already enjoy all the autonomy they need may relieve adults of demanding obligations, but that assertion is ultimately a profound form of child neglect. Children cannot raise themselves.[28]

The Hafens claim that children's autonomy is "little more than a façade" and their argument pits the needs and interests of children against the needs and interests of the adults who are responsible for their care (one suspects that they are thinking primarily of mothers). Those who desire to advance certain freedoms for children are merely trying to abdicate their responsibilities to provide nurture and education. They write, "To confer the full range of choice rights [voting, marrying, religious preference, education] on a child is also to confer the burdens and responsibilities of adult legal status, which necessarily removes the protection rights of childhood."[29] It can be countered that in the United States today, children do not "enjoy" this range of choice rights, and that fact has not stemmed a troubling trend to treat many youths as if they are adults. In the juvenile court system, for example, more and more children are tried and sentenced as though they were adults.[30] Restricting political rights is certainly no guarantee that families, churches, or governments will necessarily be moved to assure the economic rights of adequate food, shelter, health care, or education. And it is unclear why, if the picture of adults and their self-interest painted by the Hafens is accurate, these same self-serving adults are best suited to make decisions on behalf of children and to guide them toward maturity.

It is true that children cannot raise themselves. What the Hafens fail to mention in their critique of children's rights is that the *CRC* frames the existence of such rights and indeed the individual child, in the context of the family. The *CRC* in no way envisions an "untutored, unguided" child as the ideal. According to the preamble, "the family, as the fundamental group of society and the natural environment for the growth and well-being of all its members and particularly children, should be afforded the necessary protection and assistance so that it can fully assume its responsibilities within the community." The *CRC* also claims right at the outset that "the child, for the full and harmonious development of his or her personality, should grow up in a family environment, in an atmosphere of happiness, love and understanding."[31]

Practical theologian Pamela Couture has been among the most articulate in addressing the charges leveled by children's rights critics:

> The United Nations Convention on the Rights of the Child promotes a vision of a child who is well connected to his or her family, community, and nation, and their resources. A child has the fundamental right to remain connected to the multiple systems in his or her ecological web.[32]

Children's rights as individuals are primarily the responsibility of families. Children, like all people, can only begin to exercise their autonomy in any meaningful way when they are grounded in a secure network of relationships.[33] The requirements of the *Convention on the Rights of the Child* "do not imagine children's rights *against* family and community." As Couture reads the *CRC*, "children's rights are not understood individualistically, but communally, so that countries ensure that children are anchored and protected within their families and communities."[34] The *Vatican Charter of the Rights of the Family* makes a similar point: "The rights of the person, even though they are expressed as rights of the individual, have a fundamental social dimension which finds an innate and vital expression in the family."[35]

Families ought to be able to provide for their children and should be given assistance when unfavorable economic conditions prevent them from doing so. Again we turn to Couture's assessment of the situation of poor children:

> In some countries around the world, especially those that are poorest, adults claim to be well connected to both their biological children and their non-

biological children but claim that social conditions, including economic policy and political instability, prevent children's adequate care.[36]

Families and communities that care deeply for children need assistance in the arduous task of providing material care and education. Such assistance is not intended to usurp the functions of parents and families. Article 5 of the *CRC* states, "States Parties shall respect the responsibilities, rights and duties of parents or, where applicable, the members of the extended family or community as provided for by local custom, legal guardians or other persons legally responsible for the child, to provide, in a manner consistent with the evolving capacities of the child."[37] One practical consequence of this claim is that only when it is judged in the best interests of the child should the authorities separate a child from one or both of his or her parents, as in custody agreements or cases of abuse and neglect.[38] The child's economic rights are the first responsibility of the family. Even in the case of the political rights, where parental control and influence are circumscribed, the UN relies on parents and families to guide children in the exercise of these rights.[39]

Couture's reading of the *CRC* and her insistence on its recognition of children's "ecological web" builds on her previous analysis of the situation facing children in modern societies (both the children of the poor and the wealthy). Couture has noted a "poverty of tenuous connections" that characterizes the lives of many children today.[40] While she notes that families in some of the poorest parts of the world feel a deep connection to their own children and the children in their communities, they often lack the resources they need to respond to that connection and the obligations it imposes. In other circumstances, children's relationships are much more tenuous, that is to say that they have been weakened or "spread thin" to the point that they can no longer adequately nurture children. This may be exemplified in the rise of "absentee fatherhood" but may also been seen in economic conditions that force families to move from stable networks of support and prompt frequent turnover among child care and teaching professionals.

As a consequence, children who may enjoy more secure access to basic goods and even luxuries may experience fragility in their relationships with adults and other peers. This in turn diminishes children's social capital and access to other strands in their web (political, ecclesial, etc.). Couture states,

> Clearly, strong institutional relationships in communities support fragile families while weak institutional relationships leave fragile families to fend for themselves. Children in all family structures can be supported by strong and accessible child care, schools, activities for children, mentors, and job opportunities.[41]

She goes on to note that religious groups can play a vital role in meeting many of these needs for wider networks of family support. Unfortunately, a consumer culture gone global exacerbates this fragility, contributing to unsubstantial relationships based on patterns of consumption and making some people and relationships expendable. Couture's insights into the many forms of poverty facing children is perhaps our first indication that a rights-based approach and a family-centered approach need not be mutually exclusive and may play complementary functions in transforming consumer culture. Moreover, her analysis supports the claim that mediating institutions like churches, schools, and local businesses have a vital role to play in children's flourishing.

The Catholic Church and Children's Rights

As we have noted, the Catholic Church recognized the potential threats to the dignity of children and childhood that industrialization posed as early as *Rerum Novarum*, but nevertheless the language of rights is a more recent development. For the most part, the church has not spoken about children's rights, but rather about securing the well-being of children by guaranteeing the rights of the family.[42] This links rights (primarily economic rights as opposed to rights regarding marriage and procreation, free association, and religious preference) to the responsibilities and relationships of adults.

Concerns about rights language in regard to children, similar to those expressed by the Hafens, and recognition of the limits of proclamations such as the United Nations *CRC* also characterize church teaching.[43] If the once paternalistic approach to care for those in need is replaced by a more conflictual model of rights, without strengthening the ability of the powerless to advance their own interests, then the promise of rights seems hollow and the rich language of rights is reduced to mere rhetoric.[44] As Christine Gudorf points out, "This suspicion of rights language can be assumed to be especially strong in the case of children's rights due to the greater powerlessness of children to care for themselves."[45]

Rights language about children seems to come more easily when the magisterium enters the abortion debate. The right of the unborn to life trumps all other claims and "fetal freedom from direct abortion takes priority over all other rights of children as well as those of the parents."[46] Asserting the rights of children as they grow to maturity seems a more complicated matter. Unlike the arguments advanced in the debates about abortion, when it comes to children's rights, a good deal more control and authority ought to be exercised by parents.

As was mentioned earlier, the *Convention on the Rights of the Child* has enjoyed widespread support, and is, at least in principle, more readily accepted than other claims about universal human rights. Perhaps this is due to a general consensus about children's vulnerability and a concern to get beyond the rhetoric and longstanding disagreements when the lives and well-being of children are at stake. Commenting on the widespread activism in Great Britain, Hugh Cunningham notes, "To be engaged in the rescue of children . . . was in a sense to raise yourself above politics."[47] Who would deny that children are owed the very best we have to offer?

That is not to say that the *CRC* and the focus on children's rights have not faced some justifiable criticism. The advantages of being able to recognize the human dignity of children and the protections that are their due are undermined by an overly individualistic understanding of human rights. This individualistic emphasis is not the intention of the UN *Convention on the Rights of the Child*, which thinks of children in the context of the family, but not *only* in that context. Family members, including children, can transcend in a sense, the bounds of the family. Children are social beings and thrive in the context of a secure network of relationships that include but are not limited to families. Building connections with others outside of the family can be equally important for children's development, especially in circumstances where the family does not work toward the well-being of all of its members. Engagement in schools, churches, and community organizations provides means for such connection and participation in society. The extent to which families ought to be able to exercise control over children is limited.

While the language of rights, as it unfolds in the United Nations *Convention on the Rights of the Child*, is not antithetical to a critical role for families in the lives of children, it is certainly the case that this analysis seeks to draw attention more closely to children's human dignity as unique individuals who can make claims on the wider community and who continue to grow in the ability to take on increased responsibilities. Children therefore should have a voice in decisions that affect their lives, and in many ways it is difficult to think of any public policy decisions which do not impact the lives of children. Decisions made on their behalf ought to provide increased opportunity for children to exercise some self-determination. This is not only the challenging task of parenting, but also of public policy as well.

Children's Rights and Empowerment in the Case of Child Labor

Child labor has in recent years been perhaps the most visible issue generating discussion about how children's rights are to be defined and observed in an era of globalization.[48]

It is becoming clear that movements for children's rights have gone hand in hand with movements to abolish child labor. Much of what has been envisioned is children's freedom from wage labor (less clear is freedom from domestic service) and freedom for school and play. In the age of globalization, this has gained more urgency as new forms of exploitation arise and worldwide access to information about such exploitation is easily available.

As we have also seen, the rhetoric around child labor has been complex and objections to its elimination have consistently appeared in the historical record. The arguments have generally focused on the interests of parties other than the children themselves. Child labor is essential to the survival of certain industries, it is a legitimate exercise of parental autonomy (particularly with respect to agriculture in which work on the family farm is a value), and is necessary for children of the "lower orders" in the interest of public order. Even some arguments against child labor focused on the interests of adults, whose claims to a just wage were undermined by the availability of cheaper child laborers.

The *Convention on the Rights of the Child* reframes many of the ethical issues involving children and introduces the best interests of the child as the benchmark against which decisions impacting children should be made. With respect to work, Article 32 of the *CRC* states,

> States Parties recognize the right of the child to be protected from economic exploitation and from performing any work that is likely to be hazardous or to interfere with the child's education, or to be harmful to the child's health or physical, mental, spiritual, moral or social development.

Compliance with the *Convention* obligates signatories to establish minimum age requirements for admission to employment; regulate the hours and conditions under which children work, and penalize those who violate these laws. This shift in emphasis, from the elimination of child labor to the regulation of that labor is striking. Such a shift has opened the *CRC* and subsequent protocols to the charge that children's rights can unwittingly be a cover for the exploitation and manipulation of children by adults.

The notion that rights language in the context of work for children is open to manipulation gives further cause for concern about children's rights in themselves and whether this language is a fruitful way to talk about children's needs and relationships. We will see that the language of the common good tradition avoids these dangers by using rights as critical tools for the ethical analysis of concrete conditions of children's well-being and not as a rhetorical device that undermines the good of interdependence between adults and children.

The Distortion of Rights and Empowerment
Rhetoric in the Consumer Context

The secret of Nickelodeon's success is its core philosophy: *kids rule.* In everything that they do, Nickelodeon tries to take the child's perspective. The network has positioned itself as kids' best friend, on their side in an often hostile environment.[49]

We see here the potential distortion of rights and empowerment in a child-centered, consumer culture. Juliet Schor analyzes the format on a popular children's television network, Nickelodeon (though Nickelodeon is more than a television network and includes a wide range of toy, clothing, and food endorsements as well). She notices a theme of kid empowerment that is combined with edgy programming material that has the effect of "undermining mutual respect between parents and children." Schor describes the programming at Nickelodeon as "antiadultism" or "an antiauthoritarian us-versus-them sensibility that pervades the brand."[50] Parents and other adults including teachers, coaches, and neighbors are portrayed as incompetent, negligent, and even hostile to the child characters in the programming. Only the kids have the intelligence and savvy to navigate the waters of home, school, and neighborhood. Adults are not on the side of children, but Nickelodeon is. Nickelodeon can give children and young people what they desire, what is "cool." Parents just don't understand.[51] We must be cautious about what at first blush appears to be respect for children:

> Whatever the moral foundation of this modern respect for children's capacities, the media's interest in the subject has hardly been selfless. Advertisers knew that empowered children could make better consumers than dependent, compliant ones, and they were naturally attracted to media content that could advance that cause.[52]

This strategy may indeed connect with young people's feelings of isolation, being misunderstood, and being pressured by peers to fit in. However, it encourages a further separation between children and those adults who are deeply concerned about children's well-being. It also gives more credence to the notion that children are simply smaller adults and gives license to advertise to them vigorously. James McNeal writes on the front page of his handbook for advertising to children, "*Being a consumer in our nation is a right. Being a marketer is a privilege.*"[53] The second part of this claim, which may suggest the need for responsible marketing practices, is all too often obscured by the first. According to Diana Carradine, executive director of Concerned

Children's Advertisers, a Toronto-based marketing agency oriented toward socially responsible advertising, "It is each family's choice to buy or not to buy. . . . Advertising is about respect and choice."[54] We have already noted the industry's tendency to deflect responsibility for the consequences of advertising onto parents. Carradine's position though also links advertising to children to rights rhetoric, particularly as it takes shape in North American discourse; it is all about respecting and enhancing individual choice.

Schor notes that some advertisers claim that even the current levels and types of advertising are too restrictive and protective of children. Not only do the advertisers have a right to free expression in their ad spots (though whether advertisements are protected free speech is debatable), some argue that the children have a right to be advertised to, they have a right to know about what is available for purchase.[55] This is a complete distortion of the potential for children's rights language to analyze and critique current market practices and to secure minimum levels of well-being for all children, in favor of a limited rhetorical use of the concept of rights that is not meaningfully connected to obligations on the part of adults to secure well-being.[56]

Children's real liberation and empowerment are not achieved by undermining the interest that adults have in raising and educating children. Portraying parents and teachers as foolish does not advance the cause of children. Pitting the real interests of parents and children against each other does little to serve the cause of exploited children. Indeed, a Christian perspective, to the extent that it seeks children's liberation from exploitation by adults, needs to critique such an impoverished view of children's empowerment. Children are empowered when they are able to participate with adults in the communities of which they are a part and in ways that serve individual and communal flourishing.

Children and a Focus on the Family

As we have seen in the above discussion of children's rights, many who advocate for children envision children in the context of the family. The United Nations *Convention on the Rights of the Child,* while it clearly draws attention to the unique personhood of each individual child, recognizes that the best place from which to exercise individual rights, both economic and political, is a loving family relationship. Among children's rights is in fact a right to be meaningfully connected to family, community, a faith tradition, and culture. Similarly, in the teachings of the Catholic Church "children's interests were understood to be protected and promoted through defense of the rights of the family."[57] Unfortunately an exclusive focus on the family can obscure the reality of individual children in those families, as well as children who do not find themselves in families that care for them well or, for that matter, who do not find themselves in families at all. An adequate public policy and responsible ethical teachings will take these children into account.

We cannot assume that attention to families always works in the best interest of children, especially poor children. As we saw in the lives of Iqbal Masih and other children in carpet factories who worked to pay a family debt or to ease the financial burden of having girl children, children's basic well-being can be undermined by family strategies. It is understandably difficult to imagine a better future for one's children in the daily struggle for survival. A recent article in the *Boston Globe* illustrates the tension between children's contribution to family well-being through work as at once an expression of fidelity and work that clearly undermines children's well-being in the context of grinding poverty. In the mining town of Potosi in Bolivia, children labor beside their parents in mines. Not unlike the chimney sweeps of another century, children's size makes them likely candidates to be miners. They crawl into small, dark shafts in order to place and detonate explosives. This work is clearly dangerous for the children and the adults, many of whom suffer the loss of fingers, eyesight, and are vulnerable to serious respiratory illness. They work for an inhumane wage. The children are unable to attend school. The parents need the help of the children in order to support their families and have despaired of education's ability to raise them out of poverty. The reporter writes, "Persuading parents to sacrifice a child's vital income for a hypothetical better future is a hard sell." This is not due to the callousness or cruelty of parents. There simply are no other options for meeting the basic needs of survival.[58]

Yet, acknowledging these realities need not imply that all forms of work undertaken to support families are acceptable. In the ideal, breadwinners should earn a family living wage that would allow children to pursue education and continue to live faithfully in their family relationships in ways that do not threaten their life and health. Keeping families out of poverty is surely a first step, but children's claim on our solidarity and protection does not arise from their membership in families. This concern is particularly acute in circumstances where girl children make sacrifices even when there is access to resources (for example, when education, food, clothing, etc., go to their brothers).

This leads us to another caution about family-centered approaches. The model of the family that is at work in these approaches must undergo critical scrutiny. Indeed the phrase "Focus on the Family" is the name of a powerful political organization that advocates a very traditional version of "family values," among them a patriarchal family form, an emphasis on children's obedience to parents as a primary virtue, and corporal punishment as a means of discipline.[59] It may be argued that the United Nations' image of the family is informed by an appreciation of the wide variety of family forms, kinship networks, and patterns existing in the many cultures of the world. The Catholic Church on the other hand, in spite of its universal reach and claim that families are communities of love and schools of solidarity, assumes a distinctive model of family life: "a hierarchically ordered social unit under the headship of the husband with children subordinate to parents."[60] This assumption is a major weakness of the family-centered approach. Christine Gudorf is forceful in her critique:

> Today the greatest obstacle to the further development of social teaching around the rights of children is the romanticism that masks the refusal of the magisterium to analyze its model of the family.[61]

Feminist theologians and ethicists have long criticized the patriarchal family for the ways in which it undermines the dignity of women by circumscribing their social roles to those of wife and mother whose primary obligations are to obey and serve. This romanticism about family life has set impossible ideals for women with regard to the care of children and household and has resulted in self-understanding that is rooted primarily in the sacrifice of self. This vision has often worked to undermine women's human dignity by not allowing women's full participation in public life. It has also ignored the contradiction between glorifying women for their sacrifices on behalf of spouse and children on the one hand, and failing to recognize the arduous tasks of building and sustaining a family as real work on the other.

What has received less scrutiny in the feminist literature is the impact that the patriarchal family form has had on other family members, most especially children, but fathers as well. There has been a tacit assumption that while the patriarchal family model works against women, it is advantageous to the development of children. The question shaping the debate about the family up to the present has been how to balance women's interests outside of the family with children's primary interest in having mothers at home and able to spend time and energy focused exclusively on their needs. As women began to assert themselves and reshape family roles and relationships, concerns were raised that these changes necessarily work to the detriment of children. A weakened patriarchal family, it is assumed, leaves children even more vulnerable to the self-interest of adults, though this critique is most often aimed at mothers whose choices for career or education are viewed as selfish.

Christine Gudorf, in her article "Western Religion and the Patriarchal Family," challenged these assumptions.[62] She claimed that the patriarchal family has negative effects on all family members including men and children in the family. There can be no doubt that this traditional family form has had many advantages for men, including control over family resources and access to means of personal fulfillment beyond the confines of home and hearth. But mirroring the dynamic experienced by women as wives and mothers, men as husbands and fathers are forced to fit a certain mold and live up to a set of cultural expectations that can be very limiting. Men suffer the stress of having to act as sole provider of family resources and often choose employment that is best suited to the standard of living they desire and not necessarily matched to their gifts and talents or sense of vocation. These societal expectations can also keep men from growing in the virtues of care and compassion for the vulnerable. They do not receive enough practice in the intimate exercise of caring for a very fragile other who needs to be nursed and have diapers changed.

Times are changing for men, however slowly. More men take on responsibilities in the home that are connected to the immediate care of children. The formerly sharp division of household labor along gender lines is blurring. However, it must be stated that sociological studies continue to give evidence of women's "second shift," as they take on work outside the home and remain primarily responsible for household chores and child care.[63] Men who are taking on increased responsibility for children, willingly or not, are often praised for their efforts, while this juggling act is not considered above and beyond the call of duty for women, but rather is simply the expectation. Daring to be different remains just that, daring. Creative family arrangements with regard to work, household, and parenting continue to be countercultural.[64]

These changes in gender roles and spousal relationships continue to be advocated for on the basis of the interest in the growth and development of the parents in the family. The patriarchal family has stunted the emotional life of men and their capacity for developing virtues associated with empathy and care. Oppressive family structures have undermined women's dignity and potential contributions to the wider society. But what is the impact of the patriarchal family on children? Children are often understood to be the primary victims of the "demise" of the patriarchal family and of the women's movement generally. According to Gudorf,

> Even liberals, who support the changes in women's role opposed by the right, often approach the issue of family by asking how to compromise the legitimate aspirations of women with the real needs of children for the protective nurture of the traditional family. There is little systematic attempt to assess the positive and negative effects of the traditional family on children.[65]

It is assumed that children are losing out when their mothers go to work outside the home and that they would be better off if mothers were a constant presence. Again, this view takes for granted that this picture of the traditional family was indeed a historical reality. It fails to consider that women have always worked both in the home and beyond. It also fails to consider seriously the situation of poor women, for many of whom precious time with children is a luxury they cannot afford (and may even be prevented from if they are receiving the types of public assistance increasingly conditioned on work requirements).[66] Today's working mothers may in fact be able to spend more time with their children than mothers in previous eras.[67] It is not entirely clear that children thrived in the patriarchal arrangement any more than their mothers did. This hierarchical family may even have encouraged behaviors and attitudes among children that inhibit their flourishing as human beings as well as their growth in the Christian life.

In the hierarchical view of the patriarchal family, subordinate members are called to be subservient and obedient. While many women may object to taking marriage vows that include "love, honor, and obey," obedience continues to be the basic virtue for children in the family. This version of the traditional family structure inhibits children from articulating and acting on their own interests as well as resisting abuse on the part of authority figures. Moreover, the family itself is endowed with a certain autonomy that does not allow for those outside the family circle to intervene on children's behalf. The family is a private place.[68] The isolated, private family can be stifling of children's development and also prohibits others (other families, churches, governments) from having a say in how well a family is functioning to protect and nurture particular children.

One of the most prominent limitations of the family-centered approach to children's well-being then is the romantic view of the patriarchal family that often underlies that approach. Many proposed public policies provide incentives for those who need assistance in caring for their children to fit the mold of the patriarchal family. The children in families that don't fit neatly into that box are often left out of the loop and are denied access to important resources.[69] If we are to draw on the benefits of this approach, namely its insistence on children as relational beings who thrive when they are cared for by loving families that also mediate children's meaningful connection to the wider community, then we must work with a different vision of such a family.

The personalist view of marriage prominent since the Second Vatican Council has focused almost exclusively on the couple and their love for each other as the key to the meaning of married life. An adequate vision of married life must encourage couples' "commitment to a broader community of persons, beginning with children."[70] Even where it would seem most likely to be developed in a full-throated way, attention to children in theologies of marriage and family can be found wanting. Even though there is much to criticize in the pre–Vatican II understandings of marriage and family, including its hierarchy of marriage goods, we can draw on these for their insistence that the procreation and education of children need to figure into any evaluation of married life. Ethicist Julie Hanlon Rubio is concerned that the personalist vision of marriage disconnects the couple from attention to the best interests of children and even more so from the common good of society.[71]

Christine Gudorf, always on guard for distortions of the virtue of self-sacrifice, writes,

> It is not commonly recognized that the patriarchal model of parenthood that is romanticized as sacrificial is also problematic for parental development, in that a central moral task of parenthood is coming to recognize and interact with the separate identity and interests of the child.[72]

Reflecting on experiences in her family, Gudorf notes, "We ceased to see [children] as extensions of ourselves who must participate in our search to prove our own worth."[73] Parents are deeply and inextricably connected to biological as well as adopted children. The temptation lies in annexing children to ourselves as parents and using them to prove to ourselves and others that we are successful at marriage and parenting. Julie Rubio advocates a "three-in-one flesh" approach in which children are the concrete symbols of their parent's one-flesh union and so their well-being becomes the benchmark for ethical reflection on married life and the legitimacy of divorce and remarriage. The metaphor has much to commend it, but it may limit our ability to envision children in and of themselves, as partners in the journey of family life who are also on personal journeys of their own.[74]

Another danger in this child-centered approach to family life is that it has the potential to once again turn the family in on itself, preoccupied with the well-being of its members, often at the expense of others. Anderson and Johnson note that the alternative to a "culture of indifference" is not "child-centeredness."[75] Their fear is that child-centeredness quickly becomes a controlling "over involvement" in children's lives that fails to respect children for who they are. Rubio seeks to avoid this trap. Rubio's larger project is reconnecting marriage and family life to the work of the common good. In this sense, she takes up the recommendations of Lisa Cahill in *Family: A Christian Social Perspective*.[76] Strengthening this link between the intimate life of the family and wider social networks is critical to an adequate approach to children and childhood. It would also seem that enhancing the family's connection to other institutions and networks of support may even serve to diffuse the kinds of conflict within families that often lead to marital breakup.

In *A Christian Theology of Marriage and Family*, Rubio proposes the "dual vocation of Christian parents."[77] Rather than focusing exclusively on the well-being of their own children, both mothers and fathers are called as Christians to contribute to the common good through work outside the family. In this way they become models of committed discipleship both through their faithful and lasting commitment to each other as spouses and through their respective vocations.[78] Through their parents, children are connected to other adults who share in the responsibility for their care. They are also introduced to the notion that they too have responsibilities to contribute to the good of society and to the well-being of the poor and vulnerable in particular. They can share in their parents' dual vocation by taking on increased responsibility for the household in what Bonnie J. Miller-McLemore calls the "pitch in family" and by participating in activities outside the home as well (which may include, but probably ought not to be limited to, "traditional" and competitive activities such as soccer games and piano lessons).[79] The family ought to function as a place of nurture for children and as a school for compassion and solidarity. The family is not therefore relegated to serving as a haven in a heartless world where wife and children provide refuge and emotional gratification for the breadwinning father. The boundaries between the private life of the family and the public worlds of work, worship, and community should be much more fluid than they are envisioned in our present culture.

Both Cahill and Rubio are concerned that parents' activities and indeed activism outside the home should tend toward widening the family's circle of solidarity. Christine Gudorf has noted that the experience of parenting itself, and in particular her experience of adopting a child with a serious medical condition, can invite one to solidarity with children, and with parents who struggle to provide for their children in extremely adverse circumstances. All too often, however, adults use their power to compete with others in order to secure the best possible resources for the children in their families. This leaves poor and marginalized parents and their children fewer resources and a smaller circle of allies. Reflecting on an experience in her own community, Lisa Cahill relates a story that highlights this tendency and calls on parents and families to be concerned for children who are not "their own" and even more for children and others who are marginalized.

> No dearth of community activism there. Nonemployed, highly educated mothers with lots of leisure time banded together to advocate for resources to be redistributed to "talented" children from those with "special needs" . . . and to build a new school playground with private funds after the city ruled renovations an unfair drain on a budget shared with the schools of less-wealthy neighborhoods.[80]

The temptation to expend all of one's energy, resources and influence on behalf of one's own children, children who already enjoy privilege, is very real and needs to be resisted. Connecting families to the common good and building bridges of solidarity with poor families and children is crucial, but it cannot be limited to "acting locally" without any sense of the ways in which "acting locally" can fail to meet the demands of solidarity and may have a negative impact on the well-being of others.

An adequate approach to children and childhood will need to draw upon a vision of family life that is not exclusively focused on the family as an isolated unit of social life, or on one particular model of familial relationships. Supporting "family" does not always ensure that all children receive the goods that they need to thrive. Girl children in particular may be asked to sacrifice for "family" well-being in ways that undermine their dignity as they lose out on access to basic goods like food, health care, and education for the sake of brothers or other male members of the family. The family-centered approach reminds us that children thrive in loving relationships and that society and the church should do all they can to help sustain those relationships without unduly romanticizing them. Families need to be encouraged to be schools of solidarity that invite all family members, including children, to transcend the bounds of family life.

Rights, Responsibilities, and Relationships

Those who advocate for children's rights and those who call for a focus on families have each brought something crucial to the table around which we deliberate about children's well-being. The task before us is keep their contributions in creative tension, and as I will argue, fold them into a common good perspective that accounts for the interaction between rights, responsibilities, and the relationships children need to thrive.

The concept of children's rights has called our attention to children's human dignity as individuals and "conveys that children are persons, and as such are owed the same protections as adults."[81] Such dignity is recognized and attended to by providing children with the goods necessary for their survival and flourishing. Children's basic needs include food, shelter, clothing, health care, education, and loving and secure relationships. They must be immune from the abuse and exploitation that often accompany child labor and situations of armed conflict. Moreover, children also claim rights to culture, to free association, and religious preference. The danger here is an overly atomistic view of rights. Rights language often suggests that rights belong to an autonomous individual without enough reference to the web of relationships that necessarily characterize human beings and communities. This attention to relationships is crucial especially with regard to children who are necessarily dependent on adults for much of what they need. Making a claim for children's rights also involves attention to adult responsibilities and relationships.

In addition to a focus on the dignity of each unique individual child and her claim on the community, the movement for children's rights also highlights the importance of participation. This emphasis will receive further elaboration in the following chapter. No less than adults, children need to participate in our common life in order to flourish. While we might want to be cautious about the exact nature of their participation, especially in economic and political life, but also in the life of a family, encouraging participation in accord with their increasing maturity is vital.

Children grow and thrive in families who love them and are able to provide important resources. A family-centered approach to children's well-being demands that we create a larger social environment that is truly "family friendly." Rather than focusing on the rights of children themselves, some argue for the rights of the family as the best way to secure children's well-being. The teachings of the Catholic Church serve as a prime example of this approach, yet even the UN *Convention on the Rights of the Child* envisions children as part of families and kinship networks. As the Hafens noted, children cannot and should not be left to raise themselves—even though millions of the world's children are left to do just that, raise themselves and their siblings. An advantage over an individualistic approach to rights is an approach that begins with the most important relationships in a child's life. The family-centered approach highlights the need that children have for loving families and suggests that the greatest poverty a child can face is to be without a family.[82]

As we noted, there are dangers here as well. When the family is envisioned itself as an autonomous unit that serves to protect its members from the outside world, the family can close itself off from the concerns of the common good, concerns that profoundly affect the lives of children. While this vision of family life may avoid the "tenuous connections" noted by Pamela Couture, a self-enclosed family can sometimes fail to recognize the responsibilities we share as a community for all children, even those children who are not "our own." Some parents may also be inclined to think that the security that they and their children enjoy has been achieved independently of any socially conferred benefits. Couture is clear on this point:

> My point is that strong families are interdependent with society in a variety of ways that they take for granted. They are self-determined; they are *not* "self-sufficient." Fragile families, such as those moving from public assistance to employment, should not be expected to become self-sufficient; rather they need strong interdependent bonds that anchor them to society.[83]

Strong, thick, rich connections prepare young people to initiate new connections of their own. An adequate approach to children and childhood must guard against the solipsism of family life. We must also not be naïve about the ability of individual families on their own to resist the negative impacts of wider cultural trends, including the effects of a multibillion dollar advertising industry on the lives of children.

A related liability of this approach is the tendency for families, and heads of families in particular, to think of themselves as immune from criticism from the outside. In this context abuse and manipulation of family members, most especially children but other vulnerable members as well, can fester. It is also not so obvious that traditional family forms always work to children's advantage. Christine Gudorf has pointed out that many critics of the traditional patriarchal family have focused on the ways in which women have suffered in this arrangement. What receives less attention is the notion that this family form also fails to enhance the dignity of other family members as well, including fathers and children. A focus on family needs to be a focus on *families*. An adequate family approach respects, though not uncritically, a variety of family forms and looks to the ways in which other mediating institutions can work to benefit families of all shapes and sizes. When kept in tension with a rights-based approach, the family-centered perspective can highlight the need for expressions of the virtue of care in political and economic institutions and the need for justice within families.

The market approach, or the approach of economic liberalism, is more problematic. Its underlying anthropology, which reduces persons to their roles in the arena of exchange—commodity, consumer, or burden—does little to advance the concept of intrinsic human dignity and leaves scores of people on the margins of social life. It also emphasizes the independent, rational actor (even as marketers are keenly aware of relationship dynamics and the impact of advertising on emotions and desires). This affects children, who are indeed actors in this sphere, but actors with little or no ability to resist its harmful consequences. Moreover, the prominence of a capitalist approach to social life may serve to weaken the other important institutions in a community, thereby weakening the "social capital" of children and families.[84] Even though a common good perspective will remain critical of the market's dangers, it will also need to demand that children be connected to social institutions beyond the home, including the market.

An adequate perspective must also include some economic analysis in an effort to understand how market forces impact the lives of children. Poverty cannot be laid entirely at the door of individual parents who are unable or unwilling to provide for their children. There are systemic factors that perpetuate the cycle of poverty. The market can play a role in breaking this cycle only if this important arena of social participation is set in the context of a commitment to human dignity and interdependence in a world that demands simultaneous attention to the local and the global. Children are participants in this sphere of life. Their participation however, must be shaped by a commitment to forms and levels of participation that enhance children's freedom, growth, and pursuit of worthy goals beyond themselves. Interdependence, freedom, growth, and the common good are the ends or purposes of children's participation in the economy (and of adult participation for that matter). If the market is conceived in such a way that people serve the market and not the other way around, then the market will fail to realize itself as a potential avenue for children's meaningful participation in social institutions.

We turn now to the task of constructing an approach to children and childhood grounded in the common good tradition as it has emerged within Catholic social teaching. This proposal will attempt to weave in the insights gleaned from the dominant approaches: a commitment to the intrinsic human dignity of every individual child, a pledge to work at sustaining the many key relationships and networks of support and participation in children's lives, and a recognition of the importance of structural injustices that impact children's well-being. Children are unique individuals who thrive in the context of a web of intimate relationships, and who are also agents in the wider institutions of social life.

Notes

1. In a recent article, John Wall has undertaken a similar analysis of Christian ethical reflection on child rearing. While his categories do not represent a strict one-to-one correspondence to the approaches I have identified, there are strong similarities. Wall divides contemporary reflection into liberationist, communitarian, and covenantal responses to child rearing in the context of market individualism. John Wall, "Let the Little Children Come: Child Rearing as Challenge to Christian Ethics," *Horizons* 31, no. 1 (Spring 2004): 64–87.

2. The mission statement can be found on the Children's Defense Fund's website, www.childrensdefense.org. It should be noted that the CDF's campaign to *Leave No Child Behind* is to be carefully distinguished from the programs advocated by the presidential administration of George W. Bush, which used the phrase "No Child Left Behind" to describe its legislative initiatives.

3. Pamela D. Couture, *Seeing Children, Seeing God: A Practical Theology of Children and Poverty* (Nashville, TN: Abingdon Press, 2000).

4. Hugh Cunningham, *The Children of the Poor: Representations of Childhood Since the 17th Century* (Oxford and Cambridge, MA: Blackwell, 1991).

5. Joseph, M. Hawes, *The Children's Rights Movement: A History of Advocacy and Protection* (Boston: Twayne Publishers, 1991), 24–25.

6. Hawes, *Children's Rights Movement*, 25.

7. Hawes, *Children's Rights Movement*, 151. Douglas J. Slawson, *Ambition and Arrogance: Cardinal William O'Connell of Boston and the American Catholic Church* (San Diego: Cobalt Productions, 2007), 156. Another prominent figure in the tradition of Catholic social teaching supported both federal legislation and the constitutional amendment to abolish child labor. John A. Ryan advocated for a "family living wage" to be earned by a parent, presumably the father, which would eliminate the need for other members of the family to work at wage labor. See Christine Firer Hinze, "John A. Ryan, Public Policy, and the Quest for a Dignified Ecology of Work," in *Religion and Public Life: The Legacy of Monsignor John A. Ryan*, ed. Robert G. Kennedy et al., (Lanham, MD: University of America Press, 2001), 215–40.

8. Leo XIII, *Rerum Novarum* (1891), paragraph 33. Included in David J. O'Brien and Thomas A. Shannon, eds., *Catholic Social Thought: The Documentary Heritage* (Maryknoll, NY: Orbis Books, 1992), 30.

9. Leo XIII, *Rerum Novarum*, 33.

10. Margaret Eletta Guider, "Living in the Shadow of the Manger: Mission, Ecumenism, and the State of the World's Children," *Word and World* 18, no. 2 (Spring 1998): 179–86 at 181. The encyclical can be found at Pope Benedict XV, *Annus iam plenus* [December 1, 1919], in *The Papal Encyclicals (1903–1939)*, vol. 3 (Wilmington, NC: McGrath, 1981), 170.

11. Guider also notes that the movement for children's rights, however persuasive, remains on the margins of the broader human rights debate. Guider, "Living in the Shadow of the Manger," 180–81.

12. Cunningham, *Children and Childhood*, 161.

13. A decade later at the UN Special Session on Children, debates continued to flair over sex education and reproductive freedoms, often presenting a stumbling block for consensus on a wider range of issues.

14. More information on the Special Session, which had originally been scheduled for September 2001, can be found at the UNICEF website, www.unicef.org. It should also be noted that the *Convention on the Rights of the Child* was ratified by all UN members with the exception of the United States and Somalia. The United States raised particular objections to the *Convention*; Somalia had no functioning government.

15. Kofi Annan, "We the Children," a report delivered to the United Nations by the secretary-general in May 2002. See www.unicef.org.

16. *Convention on the Rights of the Child (CRC)*, preamble.

17. *CRC*, article 41.

18. See the *Vatican Charter on the Rights of the Family* (1983) for another articulation of this concern. www.vatican.va/roman_curia/pontifical_councils/family/documents/rc_pc_family_doc_19831022_family-rights_en.html (accessed January 4, 2009).

19. Cunningham, *Children and Childhood*, 190.

20. Bruce C. Hafen and Jonathan O. Hafen, "Abandoning Children to Their Rights," *First Things*, August/September 1995, 18.

21. Hafen and Hafen, "Abandoning Children," 18–19.

22. Martin Guggenheim, *What's Wrong with Children's Rights?* (Cambridge, MA: Harvard University Press, 2005), xi.

23. Guggenheim, *What's Wrong*, 13.

24. Penelope Leach, *Children First: What Society Must Do—and Is Not Doing—for Children Today* (New York: Alfred A. Knopf, 1994), 204.

25. Leach, *Children First*, 203.

26. Leach, *Children First*, 203.

27. Hafen and Hafen, "Abandoning Children," 19.

28. Hafen and Hafen, "Abandoning Children," 23.

29. Hafen and Hafen, "Abandoning Children,"19.

30. Patrick T. McCormick, "Fit to Be Tried?" *America* 186, no. 4 (February 11, 2002): 15–18.

31. *CRC*, preamble.

32. Couture, *Seeing Children, Seeing God*, 43.

33. See Margaret Farley, "A Feminist Vision of Respect for Persons," in *Feminist Ethics and the Catholic Moral Tradition*, ed. Charles E. Curran, Margaret A. Farley, and Richard A. McCormick (Mahwah, NJ: Paulist Press, 1996), 164–83.

34. Couture, *Seeing Children*, 44.

35. *Vatican Charter of the Rights of the Family*, 462.

36. Couture, *Seeing Children*, 14.

37. *CRC*, article 5.

38. *CRC*, article 9.

39. *CRC*, article 14.

40. Couture, *Seeing Children, Seeing God*, and more recently in *Child Poverty: Love, Justice, and Social Responsibility* (St. Louis, MO: Chalice Press, 2007), 21–22.

41. Couture, *Child Poverty*, 22.

42. Christine E. Gudorf, "Rights of Children," in *The New Dictionary of Catholic Social Thought*, ed. Judith A. Dwyer (Collegeville, MN: Liturgical Press, 1994), 143–48 at 144. See John Paul II, *On the Family; Vatican Charter of the Rights of the Family*, and the National Conference of Catholic Bishops, *Putting Children and Families First* as examples.

43. Gudorf, "Rights of Children," 143.

44. Gudorf, "Rights of Children," 144. James F. Keenan and Jon Fuller have discussed the issue of the rhetorical use of human rights language in the context of the HIV/AIDS epidemic. James F. Keenan and Jon Fuller, "The International AIDS Conference in Bangkok: Two Views" *America* 191, no. 5 (August 30–September 6, 2004): 13–16, and "The Language of Human Rights and Social Justice in the Face of HIV/ AIDS," *BUDHI* 1 & 2 (2004): 211–31 at 213. Rather than using the concept of human rights as a critical tool of analysis, some activists use rights language as mere rhetoric to alert others to the urgency of their claims. This may be particularly true in the case of children's rights; speaking about their "rights" adds urgency to the many causes of children's rights advocates but it may not help us analyze the situation more carefully or create real, enforceable obligations on the part of adults. In this regard, the notion of "basic needs" may be more helpful in assessing the challenges facing millions of the world's children. See Drew Christiansen, "Basic Needs: Criterion for the Legitimacy

of Development," in *Human Rights in the Americas: The Struggle for Consensus*, ed. Alfred Hennelly and John Langan (Washington, DC: Georgetown University Press, 1982), 245–88.

45. Gudorf, "Rights of Children," 144.

46. Gudorf, "Rights of Children," 144 and 145.

47. Cunningham, *The Children of the Poor*, 10.

48. William E. Meyers, "The Right Rights? Child Labor in a Globalizing World," *The Annals of the American Academy of Political and Social Science* 575, no. 1 (2001): 39.

49. Juliet B. Schor, *Born to Buy: The Commercialized Child and the New Consumer Culture* (New York: Scribner, 2004), 52.

50. Schor, *Born to Buy*, 52 and 180.

51. This strategy is considered "kid-centric." It is successful because it is geared toward satisfying its target audience. It is closely linked to the "branding" strategy in which all the programming is geared toward kids, not just one program but an entire channel for kids in which all individual programs fit the overall vision of the product as essentially being "a place for kids." Valerie Crane and Milton Chen, "Content Development of Children's Media," in *The Faces of Televisual Media: Teaching, Violence, Selling to Children*, ed. Edward L. Palmer and Brian M. Young (Mahwah, NJ: Lawrence Eerlbaum Associates, 2003), 55–81 at 70. Crane and Chen's work is an example of a positive view of children's programming; quality educational and entertaining programs that benefit from sound research can serve children's well-being and can serve as examples of social responsibility on the part of media corporations. Another contributor to the Palmer and Young volume brings a critical eye to the deliberate choice of "kid" with respect to programming and advertising. Young writes, "The words *children* and *child* are rarely if ever used. Instead, these little people were *kids*. *Kids* and *children* are not the same, and the connotations are very different. Children go to school and wash regularly. They are dutiful and eat their vegetables. They are born pure and need to be protected from the sinful adult world. Kids, on the other hand, are junior anarchists! They make a lot of noise, don't ever sit still, and play tricks with grownups as their victims. . . . Kidhood (as opposed to childhood) is a wild and free time, and kids have license to do what they want until responsibility comes along." Brian M. Young, "Issues and Politics of Televisual Advertising and Children," in Palmer and Young, *The Faces of Televisual Media*, 327–46 at 333. Palmer similarly notes, "Whereas children are perceived as potential victims of advertising and marketing, who therefore need protection, kids are perceived as streetwise, savvy, and quite ready for the ad-filled marketplace." Edward L. Palmer, "Realities and Challenges in the Rapidly Changing Televisual Media Landscape," in Palmer and Young, *The Faces of Televisual Media*, 361–77 at 375.

52. Kay S. Hymowitz, "The Contradictions of Parenting in a Media Age," in *Kid Stuff: Marketing Sex and Violence to America's Children*, ed. Diane Ravitch and Joseph P. Viteritti (Baltimore: Johns Hopkins University Press, 2003), 228.

53. James U. McNeal, *Kids as Customers: A Handbook of Marketing to Children* (New York: Lexington Books, 1992); italics in text.

54. Cited in Sabita Majib "Watch Out . . ." *The Hindu Business Line*, June 10, 2005, www.thehindubusinessline.com (accessed June 11, 2005).

55. Susan Linn, *Consuming Kids: The Hostile Takeover of Childhood* (New York: The New Press, 2004), 150–51.

56. Keenan and Fuller, "The International AIDS Conference in Bangkok," 13–16; and "The Language of Human Rights and Social Justice in the Face of HIV/AIDS," 211–31 at 213.

57. Gudorf, "Rights of Children," 144.

58. Indira A. R. Lakshmanan, "In Danger's Way: Trapped in Cycles of Poverty, Children Toil in Bolivia's Mines," *Boston Globe*, June 26, 2005, A1, A10.

59. Information on Focus on the Family can be found at www.family.org (accessed May 16, 2009).

60. Gudorf, "Rights of Children," 144.

61. Gudorf, "Rights of Children," 145.

62. Christine E. Gudorf, "Western Religion and the Patriarchal Family," in Curran, Farley, and McCormick, *Feminist Ethics and the Catholic Moral Tradition*, 251–77.

63. See Arlie Russell Hochschild, *The Time Bind: When Work Becomes Home and Home Becomes Work* (New York: Henry Holt and Co., 1997); and with Anne Machung, *The Second Shift* (New York: Avon Books, 1990).

64. For an account of the need for greater gender justice within the family setting see Susan Moller Okin, *Justice, Gender, and the Family* (New York: Basic Books, 1989). For an integration of the need for justice within families and the need for the virtue of care in wider social networks see Mary Stewart van Leeuwen, Annelies Knoppers, Margaret L. Koch, Douglas J. Schuurman, and Helen M. Sterk, *After Eden: Facing the Challenge of Gender Reconciliation* (Grand Rapids, MI: Eerdmans, 1993), 416–51.

65. Gudorf, "Western Religion," 266.

66. Thomas Massaro, *Catholic Social Teaching and United States Welfare Reform* (Collegeville, MN: Liturgical Press, 1998), 71–77.

67. Gudorf, "Western Religion," 267. While this may be true, it may also play into the debates about "quality" time with children over "quantity." Parents with access to adequate, even superior, child care are freed to be with children for play and emotional satisfaction without having to be the primary disciplinarians or educators.

68. It should be noted that the principle of subsidiarity in the Catholic tradition, which provides protection for families from interference on the part of the state, also allows such interference when individual members of the family are threatened. Subsidiarity highlights both the autonomy and interdependence of social institutions like the family, the church, national governments, and international bodies.

69. There is an important caveat here. Poor families, often headed by women without the active presence of a husband or father, are not encouraged to live up to this ideal in the same way that middle class families are. For families with access to resources, the presence of the mother as primary nurturer is crucial for children's upbringing. Fathers are encouraged to be responsible and faithful wage earners and mothers are called to return from professional work to the home. Poor women who receive public assistance are required to do just the opposite. They must work outside

the home as a condition for receiving benefits and are often forced to rely on less than adequate child care.

70. Julie Hanlon Rubio, "Three-in-One Flesh: A Christian Reappraisal of Divorce in Light of Recent Studies," *Journal of the Society of Christian Ethics* 23, no. 1 (Spring–Summer, 2003): 47–70 at 53.

71. Rubio, "Three-in-One Flesh," 53.

72. Christine E. Gudorf, "Sacrifice and Parental Spiritualities" in *Religion, Feminism, and the Family*, ed. Anne Carr and Mary Stewart van Leeuwen (Louisville, KY: Westminster John Knox Press, 1996), 294–309 at 303.

73. Gudorf, "Sacrifice," 298.

74. Rubio's reflections on parenting her three boys reveals that this recognition, while not obvious in the three-in-one flesh metaphor, is very much a part of her real life experience.

75. Herbert Anderson and Susan B. W. Johnson, *Regarding Children: A New Respect for Childhood and Families* (Louisville, KY: Westminster John Knox Press, 1994), 28.

76. Lisa Sowle Cahill, *Family: A Christian Social Perspective* (Minneapolis: Fortress 2000), 135–37.

77. Julie Hanlon Rubio, *A Christian Theology of Marriage and Family* (Mahwah, NJ: Paulist Press, 2003), 89–110.

78. One possible drawback of this proposal is that the kinds of work that parents do needs to embody Christian values. Not all work can be considered consistent with this vocation.

79. Bonnie J. Miller-McLemore, *Let the Children Come: Reimagining Childhood from a Christian Perspective* (San Francisco: Jossey-Bass, 2003).

80. Cahill, *Family*, 12.

81. Todd David Whitmore with Tobias Winright, "Children: An Undeveloped Theme in Catholic Teaching," in *The Challenge of Global Stewardship: Roman Catholic Responses*, ed. Maura A Ryan and Todd David Whitmore (Notre Dame, TN: Notre Dame University Press, 1997), 162.

82. Thanks to Margaret Eletta Guider, who offered this insight in a personal conversation.

83. Couture, *Child Poverty*, 72. In this she refers to her previous work, *Blessed Are the Poor? Women's Poverty, Family Policy and Practical Theology* (Nashville, TN: Abingdon Press, 1991).

84. Robert D. Putnam, *Bowling Alone: The Collapse and Revival of American Community* (New York: Simon and Schuster, 2000).

3

Children and the Common Good

O UR EXPLORATION OF THE REALITY OF CHILD LABOR and the evolving efforts to
end it introduced us to Craig Kielburger, a young Canadian boy moved
to action by the plight of one particular child in Pakistan, Iqbal Masih. We
attend to Craig's experience again, because he is an example of children's active participation in the common good and the option for the poor and the
cultural assumptions that strain against such participation. Interestingly, as
Craig was trying to raise awareness about the plight of child laborers, some
of the media focus was instead directed at him personally because he con-
founded assumptions about young people's agency and their potential for
social participation in building a just society. Craig was amazed to find that
many adults in Western, industrialized contexts did not think he was a "normal" teenager. He writes,

> At thirteen . . . I should be thinking about sex and girls, and not about human
> rights or child labour. Others have asked me if I feel I have lost my childhood,
> since I have become so caught up in the fight against child labour.[1]

It might be truer to say that Craig had gained a new sense of the possibilities of childhood in his struggle to eliminate child labor. It is possible to play
and enjoy friends, family, and school without losing a sense of solidarity
with other children in the world. It may even be possible to do these and to
contribute to the family's financial well-being. Some adults could not help
but see in Craig a pawn for the political self-interests of adults who exploited
his passion for a just cause because "normal children" should not want to

take on such responsibility. A picture of the child as a contributing member of a family (who provided significant support for his journey) that orients itself toward the common good of society might go a long way to correcting this distorted vision in which children of privilege are or should be simply self-involved and unmotivated by injustice. While we should rightly applaud Craig's continuing work on the part of children and young people, we might ask ourselves why we think of him as an anomaly or as extraordinary. Might this tendency limit what we expect of children in our lives and our sense of responsibility for providing both encouragement and access to avenues of participation particularly among children who are marginalized?

Robert Coles, widely respected for his scholarship on the moral and spiritual lives of children, highlighted other examples of the engagement of children in our nation's history in his book *Children of Crisis: A Study of Courage and Fear* (1967). Children and young people were deeply involved in the civil rights movement in the south. He reflects on how remarkable it was for these young people to be "initiating such responsible, nonviolent protests, to be leaders in social change." According to Coles, "modern history has no precedent for children directly involving themselves in an attempt to change the social and political structure of the adult."[2] In the case of children in the civil rights movement, we have children facing tremendous risk in order to bring about justice for the common good. Some might argue that this was the work of manipulating adults; children ought to be protected from such involvement. But for Coles, such "protection" only leads to further exploitation and the internalization of racism and oppression:

> When we find out what happens to them if they don't protest, we will find out about children in daily subjection who have been asked to forfeit their freedom by the decision that they must endure tyranny rather than face "danger" or "trauma," and do so at a time when that endurance hardly seems a necessity.[3]

Ruby Bridges and the Little Rock Nine stand as provocative images of young people willing to stand up for justice and the common good, and reveal "by the contrast that they make" the failure of society to secure the safety and well-being of its most vulnerable young people. Their witness reverberates in history and continues to make claims on the community.[4]

Georg Sporschill, reflecting on his experiences working with street children in Rumania, makes a similar claim and extends the notion of agency for young people to a desire to act in a particular way, as ministers:

> The most important point is that the children . . . look for security, a family and even more a role. They want to minister, serve, take on a role in the world and also have a role before God, to serve God. The devotion and piety with which

they do this leaves no doubt about this human longing which is so manifest in our children.[5]

Claims about childhood vulnerability, and even some calls for increased protection, do not necessarily enhance the recognition of children's human dignity. Recognition of their human dignity may be more effectively accomplished by encouraging the engagement of children and young people in political, social and ecclesial life, in ways that are free from exploitation. The participation of children and young people in the common good and the struggle for justice may be fostered in the home but it must also be welcomed and encouraged at the many levels of civil society including schools, churches, governments, nongovernmental organizations, and international bodies. The voices of these children who claim full, interdependent membership in the many overlapping communities of which they are a part guide a Christian perspective grounded in the common good. In this way they challenge Christians to articulate what they hope for the children in our families, in our communities, and across the globe.

Common Ground between Individual Rights and Family Values

The challenge of formulating an adequate approach to children's needs involves integrating the benefits of the previously explored rights-based and family-centered models while mitigating their liabilities. These liabilities often stem from inadequate anthropologies, or visions of the child in the picture as a person. The portrayal of children that is advanced by a Christian perspective grounded in the common good will need to be more complex than viewing children as either economically burdensome or emotionally priceless. As we saw earlier, these images fail to capture the full picture of children in our experience and they limit our ability to form an adequate vision of a fulfilling childhood. They have the potential to romanticize some children and demonize others. Images of the innocent child, the burdensome child, the hurried child, the child consumer, the commodified child, and the emotionally priceless child do little to generate creative ways to understand our responsibilities toward the children in our own families and toward "other people's" children. Yet these are the images that continue to shape the debates about issues facing children.

We have examined the potential contributions and liabilities of family-centered and rights-based approaches to securing children's well-being. The children's rights approach, which emphasizes children's human dignity as unique individuals in their own right, may be susceptible to the charge of reflecting a radical individualism which fails to recognize the key relationships that enhance flourishing and may fail to fully protect vulnerable children from exploitation. Building on the analysis of Pamela Couture, I have argued that the *Convention on the Rights of the Child*, the key document for a children's rights perspective, avoids this danger by situating children within the context of family and community.

The family-centered approach tends toward the other end of the spectrum. Profoundly aware of children's dependence on adults and their existence in a network of relationships, this perspective too often relies on an inadequate model of the family (namely the patriarchal, private family) and may fail to fully recognize children's interests, especially when those interests conflict with the interests of adults. This approach may be too confident in the family's ability to withstand social pressures that threaten the well-being of its members. The family-centered approach also neglects the very real and pressing needs of children in families that do not fit the traditional model of breadwinning father and stay-at-home mother. Lastly, this approach may not account well for the many children who no longer find themselves in functioning families even as it highlights children's need for a family environment.

In some sense, both the rights-based and family-centered approaches share a resistance to the influence of market logic on the lives of children, though determining the extent to which they challenge the underlying assumptions of market rationale is more complex. An adequate approach will surely need to address the impact of economic forces on the lives of children and will need to challenge the many ways in which market capitalism can distort the picture of the human person and overextend its proper sphere of influence. The market approach often reduces children merely to their function as consumers or as sources of inexpensive labor. In the context of globalization, this situation becomes increasingly grave for millions of the world's children. Children, who do not or cannot exert influence over their parents' resources, often because their parents lack adequate resources for the care of children, are viewed as burdens not only on families but on the larger society as well. Such an approach is unable to incorporate some of the fundamental commitments of Catholic social teaching, namely intrinsic human dignity, justice, and the preferential option for the poor. It is also in this market perspective that we see most readily the negative impact of the dominant, though conflicting portrayals of children operating in our culture: the innocent child whose dreams come true in the protected world of Disney and the savvy, streetwise kid ready for intense advertising.

Other images have been offered by those committed to children's well-being: children as gifts, as our hope for a better future, as strangers in need of welcome, as messengers of God's kingdom, as mystery, and partners in

God's covenant.[6] These also may fall victim to romanticism or distortion in particular cultural contexts. For example, Bonnie Miller-McLemore notes the potential pitfalls of thinking of children as gifts in a highly consumerist, materialistic culture.[7] Part of her concern is that consumer culture has lost the sense of children as gifts from God. Rather they are "artifacts to be produced, owned, managed, cultivated, and invested."[8] These are terms the market understands. We might take her critique in a slightly different direction. When we do talk about gifts in a consumer culture, we are not talking about the rich, faith formed sense to which Miller-McLemore is calling us. Gifts in this context are objects of exchange and are rarely given or sought after without unrealistic expectations about the personal fulfillment they will bring. Gifts have become something we deserve. When we are disappointed with a gift, we exchange or return it. If we are to reclaim a view of children as gifts from a loving God, we must challenge these prevailing notions of gift giving or we will remain stuck in market logic, legitimizing it using religious language. According to Miller-McLemore,

> From adults around them, children require in return unearned "gifting," without which they will not survive, demanded simply because of what children are in and of themselves. A genuine gift creates an ongoing relationship because a gift leaves a disequilibrium that suggests the hope that sharing gifts will continue *ad infinitum*.[9]

Even thinking about children as our hope for the future can be distorted in a culture where children can be pressed into fulfilling adult hopes for bright, athletic, successful children. Adults can be tempted to live vicariously through the success of their offspring.[10] A child's abilities and achievements become a testimony to a parent's worth and aptitude.[11] An adequate approach to guiding public policy that affects children will need to work first with a richer picture of children themselves, one that is both truer to the experiences of real children and one that challenges adults to reimagine their responsibilities and relationships in light of those experiences.

Perhaps Miller-McLemore's thesis comes the closest to what is envisioned here: "Children need, from women and men of faith, care that respects them as persons, regards them as capable of good and bad, values them as gifts, appreciates them as demanding of serious labor, and views them as agents."[12] This chapter picks up on several of Miller-McLemore's insights but seeks to understand human personhood and moral agency with regard to children in a particularly *social* way. In this way, we can demonstrate the need for expanded roles for mediating institutions in securing the well-being of children. Children are full, interdependent members of the overlapping communities of which they are a part—including but not limited to familial, educational, economic, and ecclesial communities. The language of the common good within Catholic social teaching provides a particularly fruitful way forward, keeping a commitment to individual human rights and the value of families in creative tension.

Dimensions of the Common Good

The pursuit of the common good has emerged as central to understanding the implications of Catholic social teaching for our time.[13] It has deep roots in Christian moral traditions whether they are Augustinian or Thomistic, as well as in philosophical ethics and secular political theory. Within Christian traditions, Catholic social teaching has perhaps been the most persistent in the use of this concept to ground claims about how people ought to live together in society and address related issues about the role of governments and religious institutions. This may be due to a number of factors including the tendency within Catholicism to argue from a natural law foundation with its characteristic optimism about the ability of human reason to discern the good and the possibility that all people of goodwill can to come to agreement on basic elements of the good life. Common good language is also geared toward the transformation of social institutions; the possibility or the desirability for Christian communities to engage this type of transformation is advocated or discouraged to varying degrees across Christian denominations (and even within Catholicism itself).

While I share the perspective that visions of the common good for society can resonate across cultures and religious traditions, making space for common ground on many particular ethical challenges, this treatment acknowledges at the outset that the concept within Christianity is a profoundly theological one. The ultimate good for human persons is life in union with God, and as Augustine envisions in *Confessions* and the *City of God*, enjoying each other in God—salvation is a social reality. All of creation comes into being and is sustained by God's love and is destined to return to God. Moral considerations about how we are to live together in society are always set against the horizon of this ultimate good for human beings—eternal life with our loving Creator.

This vision of the ground and destiny of creation is further elaborated in the church's commitment to the intrinsic dignity of the human person as made in the very image and likeness of God, the *Imago Dei*. David Jensen stresses the importance of this for a theology of childhood. In our consumer driven culture, we are tempted to think of children as created in *our image*, and we are even tempted to pursue ways of "designing" children to fit that image—not just "like us" but what we imagine our *perfect* selves should be. This image of perfection is directed less toward human fulfillment in union and more toward characteristics we associate with power and privilege like intelligence, beauty, and athletic or artistic ability.[14]

Children, like all human beings, are created in *God's* image and likeness; this is the theological commitment. But, what does it mean? One theme that remains strong in the theological traditions of Western Christianity roots *Imago Dei* and dignity in human rationality. It is the light of reason in us, the ability to distinguish good from evil and right from wrong, that sets human beings apart from the rest of God's creation and is the mark of God's image. For a theology of childhood, this represents a bit of a stumbling block. Determining "the age of reason" has theological, ecclesial, and moral implications. Placing too much emphasis on reason, and then associating reason with abstract, deductive logic, tends to undermine the dignity of children who are before the "age of reason" when they are very young and who may cultivate other ways of navigating moral terrain as they grow (featuring emotions, relationships, and imagination for example).

U.S. political culture, while not necessarily making claims about God's image, has made claims about the features of human dignity and personhood that may also be detrimental to ethical responses to children's dignity. Assumptions about the nature of human dignity are most evident in debates about end-of-life care and physician assisted suicide. The dignified life is one marked by autonomy and control. Dignified persons are decision makers, free from the interference of others (even others with whom one is in close relationship) and able to pursue their chosen life course with a great (though not unlimited) degree of immunity and choice. The dignified person is in control of cognitive and bodily functions. Based on these assumptions, there can be lives devoid of dignity: suffering the burdens of disease, disability, and the onslaught of aging. It may be no coincidence that the undignified life is one that even in adulthood or advanced age has taken on the characteristics of infancy: radical dependence on others for all of one's needs and intimate bodily care.

Ethical issues at the beginning of life surface many of the same issues though in a slightly different way. Beyond the seemingly irreconcilable debates about whether human life in its embryonic and fetal stages possesses the same rights as human life at other stages of development, fertility and genetic technologies promise new avenues of control and choice in pursuit of perfection.[15] Human suffering is to be avoided at all costs as inconsistent with a dignified life. When this technological imperative mixes with free market capitalism, eggs, sperm, and even human life itself is not beyond exchange in the market.

Human dignity, rooted in the *Imago Dei* and honored by adhering to the demands of human rights, is profoundly countercultural in this context.

Human dignity is intrinsic, bestowed by the Creator. Theologian Paul Wadell reframes our thinking about dignity by asking not *what* makes us persons—with the dignity that implies—but rather *who* makes us persons. Our dignity does not redound to any one characteristic we possess. Dignity springs from being created and loved by God.[16] We may fail to respond to human dignity appropriately and allow our institutions to undermine dignity to the point that these violations are "like the air we breathe"—unseen, unnoticed, taken for granted.[17] In spite of human sinfulness, human dignity given by God cannot be revoked or alienated. Human dignity includes but is not limited to the exercise of reason as the Western philosophical traditions have defined it. The dignity of persons is also bodily, relational (and so interdependent), and transcendent—set on the goal of union with God. Vulnerability, including the vulnerability characteristic of childhood, and finitude are not contrary to dignity but are constitutive features of it. The doctrines of Incarnation and the Crucifixion bear explicit witness to the notion that the vulnerable, including children, are *Imago Dei* and indeed *Imago Christi.*

As we have seen in our survey of the many vulnerabilities of childhood, both "natural" vulnerabilities that arise from developmental differences, and social vulnerabilities, are not to be admired for their own sake or romanticized in any way. To do so is to gloss over the sinful exploitations of such vulnerability and defer just and compassionate response. Tom Massaro reminds us that this theological claim about intrinsic human dignity in *Imago Dei* undergirds the church's commitment to human rights by which communities strive to overcome unjust forms of exploitation through concrete practices.[18]

As we look to the horizon of union with God from the vantage of human history, the concept of the common good shapes our imagination about how we might know, love, and serve God and live together in society[19]—we need only recall Isaiah's peaceable kingdom as a metaphor for a world in which there is no fear or violence and in which all of creation, including the young and vulnerable, thrives. Building the common good though also requires practical moral decision making about human relationships, both personal and political. In the pursuit of the common good then, human rights instruments, like the *Convention on the Rights of the Child,* serve as critical tools by which we measure concrete conditions of well-being and insure that no person or community lives without the most basic goods and relationships needed for a human life. This approach, shaped by a robust theological imagination and practical moral reasoning that has recourse to concrete measures of well-being, can temper both individualistic rights rhetoric and a privatized sense of family values.

In the Vatican II document, *Gaudium et Spes* we read,

Man's social nature makes it evident that the progress of the human person and the advance of society itself hinge on one another. From the beginning, the subject and the goal of all social institutions is and must be the human person which for its part and by its very nature stands completely in need of social life. Since this social life is not something added on to man, through his dealings with others, through reciprocal duties, and through fraternal dialogue he develops all his gifts and is able to rise to his destiny.[20]

Every day human interdependence grows more tightly drawn and spreads by degrees over the whole world. As a result the common good, that is, the sum of those conditions of social life which allow social groups and their individual members relatively thorough and ready access to their own fulfillment, today takes on an increasingly universal complexion and consequently involves rights and duties with respect to the whole human race. Every social group must take account of the needs and legitimate aspirations of other groups, and even of the general welfare of the entire human family.[21]

The common good is described as the sum total of the conditions of social living whereby individuals and communities achieve their perfection, their flourishing, more easily. Institutions like the market serve the human community and not the other way around.[22] The common good is not determined by any utilitarian calculation in which the greatest good for the greatest number is sought at the expense of the few—which in reality often amounts to the greatest good for the wealthy few at the expense of the many poor. The individual is not lost or obscured in the context of the group but is rather welcomed as one who brings unique gifts to the pursuit of common goals and who receives the benefits of the pursuit itself and its fruits. In one important sense then, there is no "common good for children." If it is authentically the common good that is sought, then that would by definition include children. The same was said about the need for a specifically articulated set of rights for children—a declaration on human rights should suffice. In human rights dialogues, it became necessary to enumerate children's rights in addition to human rights more generally conceived because children's rights pay needed attention to distinctive vulnerabilities of childhood. How might we think similarly about the common good?

An adequate vision of the common good must account for the vulnerabilities and the possibilities of children and childhood, and bring children in from the margins to the center to insure that our assumptions about the "common" good are not distorted by the perspective of those in positions of power and privilege. With children's experiences at the center, the common good of society allows for children as individuals, as members of families and other communities to flourish. The institutions of government and civil society facilitate rather than inhibit flourishing for all. For example, about our form of democracy, Americans are prone to say that "any child can grow up to be president." This has come to mean that *in spite* of any disadvantage perpetuated by social structures (poverty, racism, or gender inequality for example), anyone can rise to positions of power and privilege. The real insight in the saying though is *a promise* that every child will have the resources and relationships they need to grow into positions of leadership and responsibility for the common good.

Gaudium et Spes brings a number of key points about the common good to relief. The first is the radically social nature of the human person. Human beings throughout the lifecycle, not merely at its beginning and ending, are in relationships of interdependence. No one is radically independent or autonomous—a feature of personhood that may be readily recognized in children and the elderly but is by no means limited to them. And so the good life for human persons can only be realized in community. The goods and goals that we seek are not purely our own but rather draw us out of ourselves to pursue the goods and goals of others as well.

With regard to children, practices of parenting bear witness to our ability to put another's needs before our own (though these needs are never mutually exclusive) and to invest time, energy, and valuable resources in the service of a child's interests and goals. Writ large, public resources devoted to children's education, health care, and recreation—though often disproportionately distributed among children—provide a similar witness. The challenge from a Christian perspective on the common good is to expand the circle of solidarity beyond the children in our own homes and neighborhoods. *Gaudium et Spes* was especially prescient about the increasing globalization of human interdependence and the need for a globalization of solidarity.[23]

This element of the common good also calls us to recognize and value the ways in which children themselves can and should pursue communal goals, beginning in the family but also extending outward in the neighborhood, school, church community, and so on, to the global sphere. At this end of the spectrum we might think of young people's involvement in the environmental movement as an example of connecting to the "bigger picture." A culture that is surprised by the likes of Craig Kielburger and Iqbal Masih, that frames childhood in terms of self-involvement, freedom from responsibility, and growth through competition fails to do justice to children and may exclude them from pursuit of the common good in the name of more shallow forms of protection and participation.

And so, while the language of the common good resonates with human rights rhetoric especially in its assertion that human persons can make claims on the community and its institutions to create the conditions for flourishing, it nuances this claim with its insistence on the interplay between rights and responsibilities. Rights, responsibilities, and relationships grounded in justice and human solidarity are constitutive elements of flourishing and so are constitutive of children's flourishing as well. The emphasis on mutual responsibilities within Catholic social teaching resonates with the contributions of people's whose cultures are traditionally more communal. For example, as African states, concerned about the individualistic tendencies in Western societies, deliberated about the texture of human rights for children in their cultural contexts in the "African Charter on the Rights and Welfare of the Child," they included an entire section on children's responsibilities.[24]

Children have a claim on the resources that are the fruit of God's creation as well as those that are the fruits of our common endeavor. The economic rights they claim include adequate food, clothing, shelter, education, access to health care. They also then have a claim to participation in the building up of those goods for their families and communities. This is an expression of children's intrinsic human dignity and response to the claims of solidarity. David Tolfree points to a difficulty in defining "participation" as it regards children. In his study of child worker organizations he notes, "it can be used simply to imply children's involvement or taking part in something without any implication of the exercise of influence, responsibility or power."[25] We can think of numerous instances of such participation in our schools and houses of worship in which children take part in programs designed by adults and often serve adult interests.[26]

Another way of thinking about participation involves having a role in planning, prioritizing, decision making, and execution of those decisions. A danger as we think about children's participation in the economy is that they may participate in ways that undermine well-being: our working examples are exploitative child labor and the child consumer. That children's participation is often marred by exploitation is a mark of human sinfulness that is both personal and social—it is not a sign that children's participation is itself problematic. Participation as an element of the common good for persons enhances well-being. The sacrifices demanded by participation must be shared and distributed according to the norms of justice which account for particular abilities within the community.

A final aspect of the common good, unique to its expression in Catholic social teaching, which serves the well-being of children by both protecting them and inviting their participation, is the principle of subsidiarity.[27] According to the principle as it has been applied to the lives of children, society must recognize the family as an institution with unique authority and autonomy—the state should not assume the tasks in child rearing that a family is best suited to carry out. At the same time, the state, together with the many institutions of civil society, has a moral obligation to aid families in carrying out these obligations and to step in when parents and families are unable to secure the conditions necessary for children's flourishing on their own or when the family environment itself undermines the well-being of its individual members. Here we see interdependence at work on ever-widening levels of social organization. Local, grassroots efforts to secure the well-being of children are given priority and can rely on the support (rather than the imposition) of larger institutions like governments and churches in reaching their goals. Subsidiarity also highlights the roles of mediating institutions in pursuit of the common good—inhabiting the space between families on the one hand and global networks like the United Nations on the other. Children's organizations can then play a crucial role as avenues for participation in the common good, along with churches which are in the unique position of occupying places at several points on the continuum.

As the Christian community has discerned the meaning of the common good for our time, it has paid increasing attention to the preferential option for the poor and the virtue of solidarity as these have emerged in theologies of liberation. As we have noted, children are vulnerable as children and are also members of already marginalized groups (according to race, gender, ethnicity, socioeconomic class, etc.). An option for the poor demands that those who are vulnerable have the most urgent claim on the community's resources. Their well-being becomes the benchmark by which we rank priorities and evaluate the adequacy of public policies. In this case, we inquire into the impact that *all* public policies have on the welfare of children—economic, health care, military, immigration policy and so on.[28] It also demands that those on the margins be brought to the center, their voices finding a place in the community's deliberations about how best to live. Their experiences are honored as legitimate sources for theological and moral reflection that leads to social action.

The dimensions of the common good that advance our analysis of children's participation in a consumer economy can be summarized as follows: an anthropology that celebrates the embodied and transcendent as well as rational features of human personhood created in *Imago Dei*; recognition of the radically social and interdependent nature of human dignity; acknowledgement that interdependence is more than a fact of human life—interdependence itself is a good gift from God; the pursuit of human solidarity as a virtue; insistence that human flourishing requires a just set of social circumstances and institutions that are familial, local and global in their reach; the just distribution of the fruits of the common good and the ability for all to participate in building up those goods according to their ability (which may or may not neatly coincide with their chronological age); access to human rights instruments that allow for critical analysis of well-being in the concrete; resistance of a utilitarian view of the "common" or "the many" in favor of an option for the poor as the measure of our progress toward the common good.

The Common Good and the Socially Transformative Family

The implications of the common good perspective on human rights and relationships demand a vision of family life that resists isolation. The family is the "first cell of society" and so exercises some degree of autonomy, but as with the autonomous nature of individual personhood, this is always for the sake of relationship.[29] Families may have primary responsibility for their members but they are supported by other social institutions in carrying this out. Likewise, families have a responsibility toward the common good. Ultimately, the family moves out of itself, building networks of solidarity.[30] No longer merely a "haven in a heartless world," the family engages the world in order to transform it according to gospel values. In order to accomplish this goal, the family itself must bear witness to just relationships. So families are called to be witnesses to justice as much as to love and care. What has received the most attention is the righting of gender inequality between spouses. As we noted in chapter 2, this call should also be extended to justice between generations.

This is not to say there are no differences between parents and children. Many have been rightly skeptical of parenting strategies that diminish these differences in which parents and children are "friends" in an attempt to renounce authoritarian models. There are real differences that must be respected in the allocation of responsibilities within the family. Yet, Christians claim that we are all sisters and brothers, one in Christ Jesus. One might add another dimension to the Galatians' baptismal formula, "There is no Jew or Greek, male or female, slave or free, adult or child, for we are all one." Paul would surely have acknowledged continuing differences between men and women, as we do between adults and children—but the meaning of those differences has been relativized in light of our baptism. We might argue further that in light of our common *humanity*, differences—which are ultimately a gift from God—do not necessarily imply a hierarchy in which children, especially girls, find themselves at the bottom. As the family itself is transformed, it becomes a place where children are welcomed and encouraged to share in ever-increasing responsibility for those they love and for all "the least of these." Christians are part of new family in Christ that not only puts gender and age differences in perspective; it also sets blood kinships ties against the more inclusive reality of the kingdom of God.[31]

One of the benefits of thinking about the family from within the perspective of social justice and the common good tradition is that such a view can accommodate a diversity of family forms. Such diversity is not a new phenomenon though many observers have lamented the demise of the "traditional" family by which they mean a nuclear family consisting of father, mother, and children. Families throughout time and across cultures have taken on many shapes and sizes and engaged various practices of inclusion. As Pamela Couture has noted, all of these forms, though some of their particular vulnerabilities may vary, require a robust network of relationships and institutions in order to thrive. The emphasis in the socially transformative family is on the family's function rather than its form.[32] Families witness to the good news of the gospel not by looking a certain way, but by living a certain way—in fidelity toward their members and in solidarity with others. The socially transformative family resists securing *advantage* for its members, particularly its children, at the expense of others. This vision of family life and vocation is however difficult to embody in a highly consumer driven culture that clearly sees the family as a nexus for consumer activity and competition.

The Common Good and Consumerism

The context of consumer culture presents us with a number of ethical challenges. Intensive advertising often promises that happiness can be attained through the purchase of some object. At the same time that advertisers promise fulfillment, they also instill a degree of restlessness. In this way, once the object is purchased, we almost immediately turn our attention to something else that can be bought. My daughter's birthday falls in November and I am amazed at how quickly we turn from the birthday gifts to thinking about Santa's approaching visit. We buy, use, use up, and discard objects of transient value even as we repeatedly seek ultimate value in these same objects. It is a rare gift that is genuinely cherished. Parents seek their own esteem in the things they can buy for their children. Our gaze is easily diverted from our ultimate good in union with God and the good that we can enjoy in relationship with one another toward material things—and this can be corrosive to both relationships and the environment.

As the logic of consumerism creeps into many areas of life, it becomes a challenge to articulate the intrinsic value of persons and relationships. Even marriage and children are objects to be acquired, as if they were accessories we use to communicate worth to others.[33] Children relate to one another through common objects or styles (and though they may be more vulnerable to advertising, in this they no doubt imitate the adults in their lives) and include or exclude one another based on these categories. Ironically, we also "protect" our children by consuming particular objects—ones that cater to the image of the innocent child: Disney characters or "classic toys" from a simpler time. The common good gives countercultural witness to this by training our focus on our ultimate good and claiming that the good life is one lived in solidarity with the poor.

Consumer culture also thrives on competition between individuals and groups. We not only seek well-being for ourselves and our children through material things, we seek *advantage* over other people's children. We choose schools and activities that not only prepare our children but those that will give them the "edge" when it comes to future education, activities, or employment. On a large scale, corporate America critiques U.S. education for ceding this edge to children in other parts of the world.[34] Less interested in securing quality education for all of the world's children, including girls, the aim is to educate American children to be productive in ways defined by the market. This often precludes the kind of education that questions existing social structures and measures these structures according to how well they serve the poor and marginalized.

The common good seeks the flourishing of all individuals and communities. Flourishing requires material goods to be sure, though they are to be received as gifts from God's abundance that will return to God. Flourishing also requires relationships grounded in justice and solidarity, neither of which fit well with the competitive nature of consumerism. Consumer culture fosters restlessness about our possessions and a disturbing inertia when it comes to action on behalf of suffering others. Children are not immune from this influence and readily answer the call to participate by spending. Advertisers see children as the key to the success of many products and advocates of the free market claim that our economic well-being (or rather the well-being of the economy) requires "consumer confidence" evidenced by sales statistics. This is not the participation and protection envisioned by the common good in which one understands one's own flourishing as deeply connected to the flourishing of others.

The Common Good and Education

How can a perspective grounded in the common good tradition counteract the influence of market logic on education? How can the image of a child who is a person, a moral agent, and a full, interdependent member of the community guide policy with respect to consumerism and education in the United States? First, a child who is a person embodied, relational, and transcendent from the beginning can never be treated merely as a means to the ends of another. Any suggestion that education should primarily serve the interests of corporate America and its shareholders fails to recognize this core principle of respect for human personhood. If education serves the person and not merely the market (as the market itself should), then it must serve the body, the relationships, and the transcendental nature of children. Even the for-profit educational institutions claim to respond to the creativity, wonder, and imagination of youth while they strive for intellectual development (measured by achievement on standardized test scores). Nevertheless, their commitment to this enterprise continues only so long as there is a profit to be made. Profit in itself is not morally problematic; commitment to children's education should not, however, be contingent upon it.

According to the common good, moral agency including the agency of children must be understood in a profoundly social way. Their ability to decide and act either in accordance with, or against, the life of virtue is often shaped by their environment and the influence of adults. Children are especially vulnerable to manipulation in the sense that they are unable to resist many marketing ploys. It would seem then that providing corporate access to children in educational settings through programming and advertising, or vending machine contracts, for example, should be severely limited. It is not the case that children's agency is necessarily improved by providing them with unlimited choices and decisions. As Rowan Williams has noted, children ought to be protected from many of these decisions and choices because they cannot adequately negotiate the meanings and consequences of these choices.[35] This is even more the case when some of the choices that are presented to students through advertising are harmful even in places like schools, which are supposed to serve children's well-being; the impact of fast food on children's health is one striking example.

Education is a public good, a common good. It is perhaps the most prominent example of a society's commitment to children. Supported by tax dollars, public education is sustained by all members of the community irrespective of whether or not they have children that use the schools, or have any children at all. Society has an interest in educating future citizens to contribute to the common good. The argument that those with grown children have already done their share or that those who pay for private education do not need to invest in the education of other children forgets that it has always been the case that others in the community support education for the well-being of children who are not their own. The community has a stake in the development and education of doctors, nurses, teachers, business people, and public servants. For example, aging members of the community without young children do have an interest in their being qualified young people committed to their care.

That the education of all children serves the common good of society also impacts the channels through which this education is financed. Though supported through taxes, the current system of taxation often means that communities whose property values are high have much more revenue to steer toward education. Poorer communities, unable to draw more revenue from property taxes are left with less for education. It is then incorrectly assumed that parents in these communities are not as committed to education or as willing to make sacrifices on behalf of their children. According to Kozol, "giving people lavish praise for spending what they have strikes one as disingenuous."[36] Alex Molnar concurs:

> Although there are mighty attempts to obscure it, the argument that no more money can be spent on schools is, at its root, really an argument that no more money can be spent on some groups of children. It is an attempt to replace the idea that all children have an equal claim on the educational resources of the community with the idea that some children are entitled to a better education because their parents can afford to pay for it. Some voucher advocates already are arguing that parents should be free to "supplement" the amount of money provided by tax dollars as proof of their commitment to their child's school.[37]

While citizens claim to care for all children, they are often unwilling to change a tax structure that keeps wealthier children in quality schools and poor children in less than adequate schools. Their tax dollars work only for the children in their communities and they resist diverting contributions to poorer children.

Such a position on public school funding is challenged by a number of themes in the common good tradition as we have outlined it including the intrinsic dignity of all children and the preferential option for the poor. What the teaching must wrestle with is the balance between a family's obligations toward its children and a commitment to other children's well-being. It would seem that we cannot sacrifice meeting a threshold level of a basic need for some children in order to maximize even a basic need of another. In other words, enhancing the well-being of the children in my family (whose basic needs are already more than being met) at the expense of even minimally adequate educational opportunities for other children is inconsistent with a common good perspective on children and childhood. Alex Molnar puts the point directly: "Real school reform requires a vision of justice—something the highest-paid visionaries at [for-profit school projects] can never provide."[38] This vision of justice and the common good is something that Christian communities can provide, especially as its commitments take root in the specific educational initiatives to be highlighted in chapter 4.

We can look for another approach to education, another view of the child/
student that strives for the common good. The experiences of educators, administrators, and students in Catholic parochial and secondary schools may
offer insight into how communities might approach the educational needs of
children in a highly commercialized culture. First it must be said that Catholic
school education (primary and secondary) is not available to many children
as the tuition rates can be quite high. I am not advocating here for the importance of specifically religious instruction in schools generally. I am considering only the perspective on the meaning and goals of education that are
articulated by Catholic school educators with a view to how they understand
who children are and what our responsibilities are to all children in the area of
education as a public good. Though many denominations within Christianity
as well as Jewish and Muslim communities sponsor schools, considering the
example of Catholic education gives us the advantage of examining a large
network of institutions with a long history in the United States and internationally. It is my hope that this view of children will resonate widely with
public school educators and policy makers.

The mission of Catholic education, as it has been articulated by the Vatican
Congregations for Catholic Education and summarized by Gerald Grace, incorporates five key principles: education in the faith; the preferential option
for the poor (especially in the populations Catholic education is called to
serve); formation in solidarity and community; education for the common
good; and academic education for service.[39] These principles provide Catholic
educators with guidance as they navigate an educational system increasingly
governed by market values. The extent to which these principles are realized
in practice, however, is another matter.

The example of Catholic school education is not without ambiguity. Recent
revelations of the sexual abuse of young children and adolescents by clergy
have highlighted the dark side of instilling in Catholic school pupils a deferential attitude toward authority. While we have criticized the corporate model
that encourages dutiful and unquestioning workers, we must also criticize
the formation of dutiful and unquestioning lay men and women, encouraged
only to follow and rarely to lead in the church. It is on this point that some
have claimed that the hierarchy of the church treats lay men and women "like
children." Given our assertions about the intrinsic dignity of children, this
polarization and use of "children" as a derogatory term is troubling. We must
recognize the potential for some practices in parochial schools to fail to invite
children to adulthood in the church with respect to its teaching and governing functions.

It is also likely the case that parents who choose a Catholic school education for their children are also every bit as influenced by a consumer culture as other parents in the society. Some parents undoubtedly think about their schools from the perspective of consumer choice. Catholic schools like public, charter, and magnet schools will compete with each other for pupils by marketing themselves and appealing to consumer demands irrespective of the kind of impact that might have on children themselves. At several points in their recent statement on the situation of Catholic parochial schools, *Renewing Our Commitment to Catholic Elementary and Secondary Schools in the Third Millennium*, the United States Catholic Bishops urge clergy and laity to engage in effective marketing of Catholic schools and to enhance development and endowment practices so that the schools will be viable into the future.[40]

Finally, the church must face head-on the impact of diocesan school closings (often compounded by the wave of parish closings) especially when they occur, as they often do, in poor neighborhoods. According to Joseph O'Keefe,

> if the contemporary rationale for Catholic schools is grounded in the values of the affluent, ethnically assimilated, suburban, secularized and generally content Catholic majority, the data on school closings are not problematic. On the other hand, if the rationale is . . . a clear and compelling vocation to provide for the needs of the poor and to foster appreciation of the human family in its rich diversity—the closing of even one school in an inner-city area is intolerable.[41]

These closings are inconsistent with the church's preferential option for the poor and often undermine the church's practical authority as an advocate for children. O'Keefe notes the "gulf between the espoused vocation of Catholic schools and their lived reality."[42] The Catholic Church in America, once a critical means of maintaining community among immigrant populations who were ostracized and discriminated against in the new world, may now be shaped more by middle class values in a consumer culture.[43]

Gerald Grace notes that the system of Catholic schools is "one of the most significant social institutions of the Church." He claims that the practices of Catholic primary and secondary education have sought to strike a balance between "retreat" and "mission," between removing itself from the profane world in order to achieve spiritual wisdom and moving outward to serve the needs of the community and bring the good news to the world.[44] O'Keefe calls the church to remember its roots in America, and to reclaim its mission to the poor and underserved in society, especially in the area of education, where religious communities were among the first to respond to poor children, children of immigrants, and children of color. He writes, "In keeping alive a legacy of educating those outside the ethnic and socio-economic mainstream, context and identity meet; the needs of the world coincide with the strengths of the organization."[45]

This concern is echoed by the bishops in *Renewing Our Commitment*, though they are also concerned to enhance facilities in the areas where Catholic schools have waiting lists and these are often in the wealthier suburban neighborhoods. The danger as O'Keefe and others see it is in the potential for Catholic parishes and their schools to become akin to "lifestyle enclaves" where they are isolated from the wider community and united by patterns of consumption rather than gospel values. The renewed quest for community in America should not come at the expense of solidarity which opens itself to a wider community.[46] Remarkably, *Renewing Our Commitment* calls for a more equitable sharing of the financial burdens of Catholic schools as they are vital to the church's mission in the nation and the world:

> The burden of supporting our Catholic schools can no longer be placed exclusively on the individual parishes that have schools and on parents who pay tuition. This will require all Catholics, including those in parishes without schools, to focus on the spirituality of stewardship. The future of Catholic school education depends on the entire Catholic community embracing wholeheartedly the concept of stewardship of time, talent, and treasure, and translating stewardship into concrete action.[47]

Many inner-city schools are still struggling to live the mission to children who would otherwise be excluded from a quality education. They too, live with many of the realities described earlier by Jonathan Kozol, namely economic viability and the future employment prospects for their students. According to Gerald Grace,

> parents and students expect from Catholic inner-city schools a form of education and socialisation which will result in much needed employment opportunities. On the other hand, the values of Catholic education, fully realised, may lead students into critical and questioning stance about the morality and justice of socio-economic arrangements and of contemporary work relations.[48]

Catholic schools cannot resist the changes in social life wrought by economic liberalism to such an extent that their pupils are unprepared for the world of work (either by not possessing important skills, or a critical awareness of the ways in which the market operates). By educating future workers, leaders, and professionals in the principles of solidarity, the option for the poor and the common good, Catholic schools can serve as important institutions of social transformation.

Some of that transformation begins in the school administrations themselves. Writing from a British context (which is also experiencing the heavy influence of market culture, but in which there are also important differences from the U.S. context in terms of the relationships between Catholic schools and the state with regard to funding), Grace highlights several examples of schools that have taken creative steps toward resisting market competition. The head teachers have agreed to share information with one another, to reach agreements about admissions policies and procedures, and to recognize some important "natural" boundaries with respect to student recruitment. Grace calls this "covert subversion of the logic and dynamics of market competition in schooling."[49] Other head teachers called on the diocesan officials and bishops to take active steps to regulate some of the competition between schools.[50] The Archdiocese of Birmingham developed a formal infrastructure by which the Catholic schools could collaborate in ways that mitigated the divisiveness created by the influence of market values. The partnership was explicitly oriented toward the common good and even took steps beyond joint programming to reach out to schools facing financial hardship. They attempted to move beyond the winners and losers dynamic of competition and in a sense cast their lots in with each other.[51]

In another case, educators made an explicit attempt to resist a particularly troubling trend: the rise in permanent exclusions. In order to survive in the context of market competition, schools adjust their admissions policies and other procedures in order to fill their schools with the "best" students and maintain a certain social reputation. According to Grace, "These pressures, and the actions of a more interventionist group of parents, have, it is argued, caused schools to resort to exclusions more frequently than in the past."[52] Students who threaten that reputation or hinder the progress of other children (and these disruptive influences are almost always "someone else's" children) are expelled. Any sense of mission to troubled youth or students with disabilities is undermined by this practice. Catholic schools "have to survive in an education marketplace where compassion does not feature among the performance indicators."[53] Again in Birmingham, schools collaborated to form the Zacchaeus Centre, a "learning support unit" for at risk students, in an effort to reduce the number of exclusions. The center strives to embody a commitment to community, solidarity, and the common good in a spirit of reconciliation.[54]

These examples demonstrate for us the ways in which Catholic education has the potential to resist and indeed transform some of the market logic that is governing education policies and practices. Clearly, they resist the notion that students and families are merely customers, or that students are a means to the end of a good reputation and more tuition-paying students. They must also realistically face market pressures and prepare their students to be critical participants in market institutions, participants who are also guided by compassion and a commitment to the common good. These educators are working from a perspective that resonates with the common good perspective articulated here. What is less clear in these examples is how the students themselves (and their families) participate in these practices of resistance and transformation. Surely children benefit from these creative approaches to a potentially dehumanizing culture, especially poor and otherwise marginalized children. The extent to which the students are agents of change in the schools themselves is not outlined in the research.

However often the Christian communities might miss the mark in striving for faithfulness to the gospel mission, Christian educators and scholars of education do hold to an anthropological vision that resonates with the proposal being made here. Thomas Groome, in an article about the distinctiveness of Catholic school education, highlights its positive anthropology of the person, sacramental view of life, emphasis on community, a commitment to passing on a shared tradition, and an appreciation of rationality and learning.[55] In practice, many public and private schools share these same values and aim to convey a positive sense of self to students, build a supportive community environment, and pass on a particular religious, cultural, or intellectual heritage. The language of sacramentality does stand out as distinctively Catholic, yet the other points of resonance lead us once again to be hopeful about making common cause across a broad spectrum of educational institutions. That children are made in the image and likeness of God and are invited to a life of virtue and participation in the common good which has yet to be fully realized in a world tainted by sin, is not new to those who have long advocated on behalf of school children from within the Catholic school system.[56]

Though the previous examples from the British context did not highlight the role that the children themselves can play in this process, educators, including the bishops, do call on children and young people to participation in social life as agents of change. The U.S. Catholic Bishops encourage engagement in political life as a moral obligation.[57] They publish a guide entitled *Faithful Citizenship* for Catholics with questions to consider as they make voting decisions. As part of this program, the bishops include a guide specifically for families that encourages the involvement of children.[58] Children and young people should be made aware of the issues that are facing our country and world and should be educated in meaningful ways of addressing these issues.

The bishops see that it is important for families, schools, communities, and churches to form children who are socially aware and active; in this way, parishes and schools benefit the community as a whole. This arises in the context of voting and other forms of political participation. This participation should also include the economic sphere as we have previously noted.

Children and young people can be encouraged to become more educated about the influence of advertising and about their purchases. Parents and children can do more to investigate the products they buy: Where are they made? At what cost? What are the working conditions for employees? What are our country's trade policies? There is some evidence that making distinctions between television programs and the intent of advertisements is linked to children's intellectual development and cannot be rushed. Older children do make these distinctions and can become more critical. Then families can together make more informed purchases.[59] Children can then contribute to the economic well-being of the family. Schools have the potential to be a strong ally in this process of education around media awareness and economic issues, not merely offering instruction on how to balance a checkbook or formulate a household budget. Schools can encourage a critical Christian social perspective on advertising and its effects on youth as well as on the workings of the economy as a whole. Schools can call their students to responsible stewardship.

In communities where Catholic schools educate poorer children who may have fewer opportunities for higher education and who may enter the work force (if they are not members of it already) at younger ages, other elements of Catholic social teaching need greater emphasis. Schools can educate children about the dignity of work and workers' rights to a living wage, to safe working conditions, to be free from exploitation (including sexual harassment) and to form associations. In this way young people are better able to advocate for themselves and for other workers to transform unjust labor conditions.

The ability for schools, even Catholic schools which claim to be grounded in this anthropological vision of the child as a person who is a moral agent created in God's image, to resist a consumer driven, materialistic, individualistic, and competitive culture is increasingly undermined. Catholic schools and churches strive to espouse countercultural gospel values of compassion and solidarity, yet they live in the culture too and are vulnerable to its subtle effects. Joseph O'Keefe writes,

> It will be sadly ironic if the schools lose their communal ethos in imitation of non-Catholic institutions that have lost a shared religious purpose and now serve a select upper middle-class clientele; institutions in which immigrants, poor people, and minorities feel like strangers. For the Catholic community, uncritical involvement in market-based reform initiatives may have a mortal consequence: We may save our schools but lose our soul.[60]

O'Keefe is very wary of market-based reforms taking hold in Catholic schools. They are inconsistent with the espoused anthropology of Catholic educators. Market values cannot accommodate the intrinsic dignity of the child or the preferential option for the poor that has often characterized the history of Catholic primary education in the United States. This logic also suggests that the Catholic community should be strong supporters of public education and should be watchful of the way that market logic impacts children in public schools as well.[61]

We have seen examples of how Catholic schools can provide an effective model of resistance to market-based reforms that may have negative consequences for children. They have sought to survive market pressures without succumbing to an impoverished view of the children they serve or neglecting to serve the children most in need of a rich communal and educational environment. Schools can also encourage solidarity and the option for the poor by educating children about consumer culture and encouraging children's participation as agents of social justice.

The Common Good and Human Work

The documentary heritage of Catholic social teaching begins with Pope Leo XIII's encyclical *Rerum Novarum* (*On Human Work*) in 1891. Since that time concerns about the status of workers and the dignity of work has been a recurring theme as the teaching developed throughout the twentieth century.[62] As we noted earlier, Leo XIII articulated a concern for children engaged in wage work at the dawn of the industrial era. Work by children per se was not the central issue. The pope was concerned with the new challenges presented by factory wage labor among women and children as societies moved away from the agricultural economies in which women and children had always participated.

In the 1961 encyclical, *Mater et Magistra* (*Christianity and Social Progress*), Pope John XXIII, wrote of work that it "must be regarded not merely as a commodity, but as *a specifically human activity*."[63] Furthermore, since work provides the means to securing a livelihood,

> its remuneration, therefore, cannot be made to depend on the state of the market. It must be determined by the laws of justice and equity. Any other procedure would be a clear violation of justice, even supposing the contract of work to have been freely entered into by both parties.[64]

> It is furthermore the duty of the State to ensure that terms of employment are regulated in accordance with justice and equity, and to safeguard the human dignity of workers by making sure that they are not required to work in an environment which may prove harmful to their material and spiritual interests.[65]

As a *human activity* work has moral and transcendent dimensions. It is an expression of, and not a limit on, human freedom. This is not to say that all persons possess the same ability to exercise that freedom. It is disingenuous to claim that people freely agree to the bonded labor of their children or to laboring for an unjust wage in dangerous conditions. Children are particularly vulnerable to such exploitation and yet working with this theological anthropology, we cannot claim that work by children is necessarily exploitative and indeed may be an expression of human freedom in relationship. To count as such an expression, work done by children should promote their flourishing and not undermine it, and so should build the common good. Children's work, no more or less than work performed by adults, is not merely a commodity exchanged in the market. It is a form of human participation in the common good of families and communities. If dignified work is essential in the pursuit of the common good, and is beneficial to human persons and communities, then we must consider when, how, and under what conditions children and young people participate in this element of human flourishing.

If conditions are such that children's participation is merely a commodity (their work as well as their access to financial resources), reducing children to objects, means to the ends of others, then such work must be challenged as unjust. Children are always human subjects, not in the sense that they exercise radical autonomy by their work (an assumption made by a capitalist marketplace that fails to challenge work perceived to have been "freely" contracted) but rather in the sense that their work is also human work that has moral meaning for the child and the community. It has the potential, under the right conditions, to add to the common good in which the child is included among the beneficiaries.

Among the concrete conclusions about work and the rights of workers that the Catholic Church has reached in light of its albeit skeletal theology of work is the right of workers to just wages and working conditions. Workers also have the right to organize in order to advance these causes. Workers enter these relationships freely, without coercion and likewise cannot be kept from admission to unions. Associations that seek to advance workers' rights in furtherance of the common good must also respect the "legitimate aspirations" of other groups as well. This principle is critical for trade unions comprised of adult members which, without a common good orientation, find themselves at odds with associations of child workers. The temptation then is to exclude these young people even from debates about regulating child labor.[66]

Operating from within the context of a common good framework then, we can find grounds to collaborate with organizations of child workers, which primarily advocate for improved wages and conditions rather than the elimination of all child labor. While these organizations vary in their goals and concrete practices, they generally support children's "right to work," though there remains concern that this "right" is another device for manipulation on the part of corporations to maximize profit. These organizations have resisted minimum age regulations in favor of attention to the unique contexts of the work and the children's abilities. Children are demanding to be respected as workers whose contributions are genuinely valued by families, employers, and rights activists. We find an example of child workers' voices on this matter in the Kundapur Declaration from the First International Meeting of Working Children held at Kundapur, India, in 1996:

> We want recognition of our problems, our initiatives, proposals and our process of organization.
> We are against the boycott of products made by children.
> We want respect and security for ourselves and the work that we do.
> We want an education system whose methodology and content are adapted to our reality.
> We want professional training adapted to our reality and capabilities.
> We want access to good health care for working children.
> We want to be consulted in all decisions concerning us, at local, national or international level.
> We want the root causes of our situation, primarily poverty, to be addressed and tackled.
> We want more activities in rural areas and decentralization in decision making, so that children will no longer be forced to migrate.
> We are against exploitation at work but we are for work with dignity with hours adapted so that we have time for education and leisure.[67]

In other instances, children's organizations have also demanded that distinctions be made (not a frequent tendency in rhetorical flourish) between the work that they do and exploitation: "We are against prostitution, slavery and drug trafficking by children. These are CRIMES and not WORK. The decision-makers should distinguish between work and crime."[68]

Researchers for Save the Children have enumerated the accomplishments of organizations of child workers:

> All have made some impact—in some cases considerable—on public attitudes toward working children. Their achievements are wide-ranging—persuading local authorities to repair bridges and roads used by children, developing and persuading schools to pilot curricula for working children, supporting neighborhood struggles for improved services, negotiating access to health care for street and working children, tackling abusive employers and negotiating better working conditions.

Children involved in the movements have come to see their struggle as integral to that of their families, neighborhoods, and all marginalized people.[69]

Moreover, researchers have found that membership in these organizations—in addition to the work itself—may have benefits for children including stronger commitment, as well as enhanced self-esteem and resilience. Though such activity on the part of children can bring them into conflict with adults who expect children's obedience whether they are family members or employers.[70]

The intersections between these declarations from working children and the key elements of the common good approach are worth teasing out. They envision children as dignified social agents who connect their needs to the needs of others in their local communities as well as others across the globe whom they may never meet. They demand access to conversation and decision making at all levels of society. They value grass roots programs that meet them where they are as well as the "decentralization" of power that is consistent with subsidiarity. They tend to both the conditions of work itself and the myriad other circumstances that impact life and work like roads, schools, and health care access, as well as the root causes of suffering including poverty.

The language of the common good provides fertile ground for addressing the signs of the times for today's children. It incorporates a profound commitment to human rights by recognizing the intrinsic dignity of the human person, no matter her age or ability because she is created in God's image. Relationships of interdependence on the individual, familial, and wider social levels enhance human freedom and are the context in which human dignity is expressed in history. Exploitation and violence distort freedom and violate human dignity. Protection and participation are constitutive of the common good for all people including children. For many children, though not all, a safe place to begin taking on increasing responsibility for vulnerable others is the family, though it ought not end there; it moves outward to include the human family. The common good perspective provides a new avenue for theologies of marriage, parenting, and family life by advocating the socially transformative family, engaged in works of fidelity and solidarity that aim to secure social conditions that facilitate flourishing for all.

Christians see in Jesus's birth in humble surroundings; his ministry to the poor and marginalized, including children; and the paschal mystery of his suffering, death, and resurrection, glimpses of God's kingdom in human history. The story of Isaiah's peaceable kingdom is told again. Our reading of the signs of the times has revealed the tragic suffering and exploitation experienced by millions of the world's children. If we believe that ours is a sinful *and* graced world, that the kingdom is "already" as well as "not yet," then we must also be alert to signs of the kingdom's presence in the midst of the history we are living. We must be attentive to the role that children are playing in the building of the kingdom and to the glimpses of transformation at the level of mediating institutions. The following chapter will highlight one particular educational initiative that espouses the anthropological commitments outlined in this common good perspective and provides a model for thinking about two of the central concerns of this analysis of childhood and consumer culture: the potential for schools to counteract consumer driven culture and the potential value of work done by children. It is to the Cristo Rey story that we now turn.

Notes

1. Craig Kielburger with Kevin Major, *Free the Children: A Young Man Fights Against Child Labor and Proves That Children Can Change the World* (New York: Harper Perennial, 2000), 290.

2. Robert Coles, *Children of Crisis: A Study of Courage and Fear* (Boston and Toronto: Little, Brown, and Co., 1967), 319.

3. Coles, *Children of Crisis*, 326.

4. David Halberstam, *The Children* (New York: Random House, 1998). Wilma King, *African American Childhoods: Historical Perspectives from Slavery to Civil Rights* (New York: Palgrave/Macmillan, 2005). The phrase, "by the contrast they make" is drawn from Robert Pattison, *The Child Figure in English Literature* (Athens: University of Georgia Press, 1978), ix, in his discussion of children in the work of Charles Dickens.

5. Georg Sporschill, "The Church as an Advocate of Children," *Concilium* 2 (1996): 89–98 at 96.

6. For examples see Marcia J. Bunge, ed., *The Child in Christian Thought* (Grand Rapids, MI, and Cambridge: Eerdmans, 2001); *Dialogue*, Special Issue 37 (Summer 1998); *Theology Today* 56, no. 4, Special Millennium Issue (January 2000). *Word and World* 15 (Winter 1995); *Interpretation* 55, no. 2 (April 2001); John Wall, "Let the Little Children Come: Child Rearing as Challenge to Christian Ethics," *Horizons* 31, no. 1 (Spring 2004): 64–87; Stanley Hauerwas, A *Community of Character: Toward a Constructive Christian Social Ethic* (Notre Dame, IN: University of Notre Dame Press, 1981); David H. Jensen, *Graced Vulnerability: A Theology of Childhood* (Cleveland: Pilgrim Press, 2005); Pamela Couture, *Child Poverty: Love, Justice, and Social Responsibility* (St. Louis, MO: Chalice Press, 2007); Bonnie J. Miller-McLemore, *Let the Children Come: Reimagining Childhood from a Christian Perspective* (San Francisco: Jossey-Bass, 2003) and *In the Midst of Chaos: Caring for Children as Spiritual Practice* (San Francisco: Jossey-Bass, 2007); Danna Nolan Fewell, *The Children of Israel: Reading the Bible for the Sake of Our Children* (Nashville, TN: Abingdon Press, 2003); Martin E. Marty,

The Mystery of the Child (Grand Rapids, MI: Eerdmans, 2007); and Patrick McKinley Brennan, ed., *The Vocation of the Child* (Grand Rapids, MI: Eerdmans, 2008).

7. Miller-McLemore, *Let the Children Come*, 88–94.

8. Miller-McLemore, *Let the Children Come*, 89.

9. Miller-McLemore, *Let the Children Come*, 102.

10. Jensen also nuances thinking about the future in overly teleological culture, always bent on going somewhere else and thinking of time in strictly linear ways. This may close us to the possibility of God's time as well as children's sense of time and direction. Jensen, *Graced Vulnerability*, 121.

11. Miller-McLemore, *Let the Children Come*, 89.

12. Miller-McLemore, *Let the Children Come*, 164.

13. David Hollenbach, *The Common Good and Christian Ethics* (Cambridge: Cambridge University Press, 2002).

14. Jensen, *Graced Vulnerability*.

15. Maura A. Ryan. *Ethics and Economics of Assisted Reproduction: The Cost of Longing* (Washington, DC: Georgetown University Press, 2001).

16. Paul J. Wadell, *Happiness and the Christian Moral Life: An Introduction to Christian Ethics* (Lanham, MD: Rowman & Littlefield, 2008), 71–77.

17. Margaret E. Farley, *Compassionate Respect: A Feminist Approach to Medical Ethics and Other Questions* (Mahwah, NJ: Paulist Press, 2003).

18. Thomas Massaro, *Living Justice: Catholic Social Teaching in Action* (Lanham, MD: Sheed & Ward, 2000).

19. Thomas Aquinas, *Summa Theologica*, Prima Secundae Partis, Q. 94, article 2.

20. *Gaudium et Spes* (*The Church in the Modern World*, 1965), paragraph 25. The document is available at www.vatican.va/archive/hist_councils/ii_vatican_council/documents/vat-ii_const_19651207_gaudium-et-spes_en.html (accessed May 16, 2009).

21. *Gaudium et Spes*, paragraph 26.

22. Massaro, *Living Justice*.

23. See the speech given by Oscar Andres Cardinal Rodriguez, M.S.D.B., archbishop of Tegucigalpa and president of Caritas Internationalis at Vatican City July 7, 2003, "The Catholic Church and the Globalization of Solidarity," www.caritas.org/upload/fth/fthecatholicchurchandtheglobalizationofsolidarity.pdf (accessed January 4, 2009).

24. Adopted by the 26th Ordinary Session of the Assembly of Heads of State and Government of the OAU, Addis Ababa, July 1990. See article 31. Cited in David Tolfree, *Old Enough to Work, Old Enough to Have a Say: Different Approaches to Supporting Working Children* (Stockholm: Räda Barnen, 1998), 47.

25. Tolfree, *Old Enough to Work*, 44.

26. Danna Nolan Fewell shares an anecdote of a Christmas pageant, emblematic of children's participation in ecclesial life, in which one child attends to the details of the infancy narrative and disrupts the adults' plan for a charming story; she insists on playing one of Herod's "hitmen," haunting the life of the holy family throughout the play. Fewell, *Children of Israel*, 105–6.

27. Though the principle of subsidiarity is distinctive to Catholicism, several Protestant ethicists have incorporated it into their analysis of children's rights. Don S. Browning, "Should the UN Convention on the Rights of the Child Be Ratified and Why?" and John Wall, "Human Rights in Light of Children: A Christian Childist Perspective"—both papers delivered at the 2006 Annual Meeting of the American Academy of Religion.

28. Couture, *Child Poverty*.

29. Farley, *Compassionate Respect*.

30. See Lisa Sowle Cahill, *Family: A Christian Social Perspective* (Minneapolis: Fortress Press, 2000) and Julie Hanlon Rubio, *A Christian Theology of Marriage and Family* (New York: Paulist Press, 2003).

31. Cahill, *Family*.

32. Cahill, *Family*.

33. Thanks to M. T. Davila for this insight in a presentation given at the College Theology Society Annual Meeting, 2008.

34. For example see the documentary film, "Two Million Minutes." Information available at 2mminutes.com/ (accessed October 31, 2008).

35. Lainie Friedman Ross has also claimed that it is not the responsibility of parents to provide children with unlimited choices or access to information. To do so is disrespectful of them as developing persons. Lainie Friedman Ross, *Children, Families, and Health Care Decision-Making* (Oxford: Clarendon Press, 1998), 10–12.

36. Jonathon Kozol, *Savage Inequalities: Children in America's Schools* (New York: Harper Perennial, 1992), 67

37. Alex Molnar, *Giving Kids the Business: The Commercialization of American Schools* (Boulder, CO: Westview Press, 1996), 173.

38. Molnar,*Giving Kids the Business*, 115.

39. Gerald Grace, *Catholic Schools: Mission, Markets, and Morality* (London and New York: Routledge Falmer, 2002), 125.

40. United States Conference of Catholic Bishops, *Renewing Our Commitment to Catholic Elementary and Secondary Schools in the Third Millennium* (Washington, DC: USCCB, 2005). While the bishops may be encouraging the marketing of schools in order to make Catholic schooling available to more families, this position does not address the competition between Catholic schools for students. Ironically, this could lead to the closing of some schools and the tendency of other schools to self-select only the students with the most potential for success as it is defined in the broader culture. See Grace, *Catholic Schools*, 189–204.

41. Joseph O'Keefe, "No Margin, No Mission," in *The Contemporary Catholic School: Context, Identity and Diversity*, ed. Terence H. McLaughlin, Joseph O'Keefe, and Bernadette O'Keeffe (London and Washington, DC: The Falmer Press, 1996), 177–97 at 178.

42. O'Keefe, "No Margin," 181.

43. The mission to immigrant populations also has a complex history in that this service was sometimes undertaken to protect Catholic children from the influence of Protestantism in the public schools. While it built solidarity among immigrant communities it may have achieved this in part by framing a threatening "other."

44. Grace, *Catholic Schools*, 7–10. One of the dangers of tending toward the "mission" end of the spectrum involved a susceptibility to cultural and religious imperialism on the part of Catholics. Grace, *Catholic Schools*, 7. Grace opts for the image "openness with roots." Grace, *Catholic Schools*, 14. Grace cites A. Bryk, V. Lee, and P. Holland, *Catholic Schools and the Common Good* (Cambridge, MA: Harvard University Press, 1993), 334–35.

45. O'Keefe, "No Margin," 193.

46. Joseph M. O'Keefe, "Values and Identity in Catholic Education: A Response to Rabbi Michael A. Paley," *Catholic Education: A Journal of Theory and Practice* 1, no. 3 (March 1998): 322–33 at 328. O'Keefe cites David Hollenbach, "The Common Good, Pluralism, and Catholic Education," in McLaughlin, O'Keefe, and O'Keeffe, *The Contemporary Catholic School*, 89–103 at 94.

47. USCCB, *Renewing Our Commitment*, "Finances."

48. Grace, *Catholic Schools*, 89.

49. Grace, *Catholic Schools*, 194.

50. Grace, *Catholic Schools*, 195.

51. Grace, *Catholic Schools*, 198–201.

52. Grace, *Catholic Schools*, 201.

53. Grace, *Catholic Schools*.

54. Grace, *Catholic Schools*, 202–3.

55. Thomas H. Groome, "What Makes a School Catholic?" in McLaughlin, O'Keefe, and O'Keeffe, *The Contemporary Catholic School*, 107–25 at 108.

56. In *Renewing Our Commitment*, the bishops note a Harvard University study that reported "Catholic school students performed better than other students on the three basic objectives of civic education—the capacity for civic engagement (e.g., voluntary community service), political knowledge (e.g., learning and using civic skills), and political tolerance (e.g., respect for opinions different from their own)." The bishops cite David Campbell, "Making Democratic Education Work: Schools, Social Capital, and Civic Education" (paper presented at the Conference on Charter Schools, Vouchers, and Public Education, March 2000), 25ff.

57. The emphasis is on political participation and the call to transform the wider culture. Children's role as agents seeking to transform Catholic education or the church at large does not appear to be part of this program. Their citizenship in these areas has yet to be fully realized.

58. The latest information on the United States Conference of Catholic Bishops *Faithful Citizenship* can be found at www.faithfulcitizenship.org (accessed January 4, 2009).

59. Tom Beaudoin, *Consuming Faith* (Lanham, MD: Sheed & Ward, 2003). This is no easy task. Beaudoin chronicles his frustrating attempts at gaining information from corporations about the sources of production.

60. O'Keefe, "Values and Identity in Catholic Education," 322–33 at 332.

61. The USCCB advocates for school choice as a right that enables parents to exercise their vocation as the primary educators of their children. What they have in mind is supporting various voucher and tax credit programs that would help to make Catholic schools more accessible to middle and low income families. The document

Renewing Our Commitment to Catholic Elementary and Secondary Schools in the Third Millennium, does not pair this concern with a call to recognize that public schools are a shared responsibility as well, even for parents who choose to send their children to private or parochial schools. In a spirit of solidarity, Catholics should also advocate for well-funded public schools as another critical element of the "right of school choice."

62. Massaro, *Living Justice.*

63. John XXIII, *Mater et Magistra*, paragraph 18 (1961). Italics added.

64. *Mater et Magistra*, paragraph 18.

65. *Mater et Magistra*, paragraph 21.

66. See Per Miljeteig, "Creating Partnerships with Working Children and Youth," *Social Protection Discussion Paper Series*, no. 0021. (Washington, DC: Human Development Network, The World Bank: 2000) and Tolfree, *Old Enough to Work.*

67. Miljeteig, "Creating Partnerships," 20.

68. Dakar Declaration—Movement of Working Children and Youth of Africa, Latin America and Asia—Dakar, Senegal, March 1998. Cited in Per Miljeteig, "Creating Partnerships," 22.

69. Anthony Swift, *Working Children Get Organized: An Introduction to Working Children's Organizations* (London: International Save the Children Alliance, 1999), 11.

70. Tolfree, *Old Enough to Work*, 48–52.

4

A Model of Resistance and Transformation

The Cristo Rey Story

Our nation is failing many of our children. Our world is a hostile and dangerous place for millions of children. As pastors in a community deeply committed to serving children and their families, and as teachers of a faith that celebrates the gift of children, we seek to call attention to this crisis and to fashion a response that builds on the values of our faith, the experience of our community, and the love and compassion of our people. We seek to shape a society—and a world—with a clear priority for families and children in need and to contribute to the development of policies that help families protect their children's lives and overcome the moral, social, and economic forces that threaten their future.

—United States Catholic Conference[1]

Renewing Roles for Mediating Institutions in the Common Good

CHILDREN'S INVOLVEMENT IN THE MECHANISMS of the market occurs along several axes and in circles that widen out from the intimate network of the family toward other arenas of organization. So resistance to the negative impact of the market as well as the influence of the logic of the market and the market as metaphor happens on a number of different levels. We can look at individual young people like Iqbal Masih, Craig Kielburger, Ruby Bridges, the Little Rock Nine, and the participants at the UN Special Session who commit themselves to working for justice, even at great personal cost. In a consumer driven society where views of childhood that tend toward conformity to an ideal, there is much needed wisdom in the adage "one person can make a difference." It recognizes that there are times when people committed to justice will have to courageously stand up and stand out. However, it is often the case that the bravest individuals have been able to accomplish change because they found themselves supported by a family or community.

We could also look to models of family resistance to market pressures. Some families "drop out" by resisting consumerism through simple living or restrict their access to engagement with various forms of commercial media (especially media with violent or sexual content). Others strive for an "equal regard" family in which both domestic work and work outside the home are valued and shared. There is no shortage in the popular literature of suggestions for how to be a good parent, how to raise happy healthy children, and how to sustain a happy marriage in the midst of the hurried pace of modern life. These approaches are surely enlivening for many families, but we have also argued that individuals and families are interdependent with a number of other institutions that make these family practices possible and might expand the potential for broader social transformation.

"Dropping out" brings its own forms of marginalization. The Christian life may be countercultural and at times, lived on the margins. But marginalization for its own sake or for the benefit, even purity, of a few may well be a temptation to be resisted. If families are to contribute to the common good, then they must move beyond the isolation that can be so appealing in the sea of consumer culture. Families cannot rest knowing that they have protected "their" children. The socially transformative family engages numerous other institutions for the well-being of all children and families.

Churches, schools, governments (from the local to the national), health care institutions, corporations, financial bodies, professional organizations, the courts, the arts, and the not-for-profit sector all need to bring children front and center. They need to ask themselves how children are involved in these institutions of civil society and how children's well-being is served or undermined.[2] Among the most obvious and critical of these institutions in our culture with respect to children are the schools, which unlike the others, purport to be specifically oriented toward children's education and well-being as their primary purpose.

New programs in Catholic education, explicitly shaped by the language of the common good, can serve as models of resistance to a consumer driven culture that stretches us to the level of mediating institutions. These exemplars do not "drop out" altogether, forming some sort of Catholic enclave (which is not to say that some Catholic schools have not adopted this "gated community" strategy) but seek to engage market realities in such a way that they serve the common good of their communities and young people in particular. In chapter 3 we set forth the limits and advantages of exploring Catholic initiatives as a model for the wider culture; Catholic parochial education does not have an unblemished history, but it does allow us to consider an alternative model of education that has a wide network and may be replicated in a variety of contexts.

In reading the signs of the times for children we noted the pressures facing educational institutions in a consumer context. Catholic schools are no less susceptible to these pressures: families who consider themselves customers who demand a certain product; addressing pressing fiscal concerns by accepting funds from sponsors whose logos begin appearing on score boards and other school materials; shaping curricula to meet the needs of industry; focusing less on mission and more on marketability; funneling energy toward constituencies with the resources to pay increasing tuition costs rather than toward communities struggling with poverty and violence. The argument here is not that all Catholic schools are models of the common good approach, though more of them surely could be. No initiative is a perfect example of the common good in action; pursing the common good is always attempted amidst compromise. So using Catholic education as a model is not without its problems. It may also be the case that some public and private schools exemplify the common good approach.

That being said, we can look to initiatives within Catholic education (which are also being adopted by other Christian denominational schools as well) that might challenge current trends that are prompted and sustained by market rationale. The particular initiative under consideration here is the Cristo Rey Network of Catholic secondary schools, which has the unique advantage of also allowing us to think in a new way about children's work, moral agency, and contributions to the common good. Cristo Rey hopes to change the world "one student at a time"; the transformations it has wrought impact students, families, the approach to providing education in poor communities, and the businesses with which it partners. One grass roots enterprise has spread across the United States.[3]

Cristo Rey: From Tacna to Chicago and Beyond

Attempts at eliminating all child labor have fallen short and sometimes meet with resistance on the part of communities in which they take place. Rights activists fail to take into account the crucial role children's income plays in the family's economic life, or the sense in many cultures that children have concrete obligations to their families. Parents are not always convinced that education will make a real difference for their children's future.[4] Short of eliminating child labor outright then, communities might at the very least strive to overcome situations in which families must choose between education and income as they address the longer range problem of creating opportunities for the educated.

El Centro Cristo Rey del Niño Trabajador, the Cristo Rey Center for the Working Child, in Tacna, Peru, gives us an example of children's rights and the common good in action at the grass roots in a context where child labor is common. Founded in 1986, the center's mission is to "dignify and defend the working child by promoting and defending the rights of children and youth." The center acknowledges the many factors at play in analyzing child work: "While the Center does not encourage child labor, we must respond to the social and economic reality which forces children to work in order to survive."[5] The center provides services to 300 children: an alternative school, job skills training, nutrition, health care, counseling, a shelter, family outreach, and pastoral care. Children and their families are not forced to choose between an income and school for their children. The reality that these children face, in all of its complexity, is taken seriously and *they* are taken seriously as people who have much to contribute to their families and communities, but who need increased support and protection from the negative effects of child labor.

The impulse to meet real children where they are, to provide access to quality education, and to respond to the financial hardships facing poor families that moved the Center for the Working Child has prompted a new network of schools in the United States.[6] The Cristo Rey Network of secondary schools combines student work with its educational program. Unlike its namesake in Peru, the network does not explicitly serve working poor children. The schools educate children in underserved urban settings where many children are poor and have limited access to a quality education. Cristo Rey incorporates internship opportunities into its educational program, combing work and study, and so it provides a window onto how Christian communities might face children's economic realities and cultivate their role in the common good. Cristo Rey recognizes the good that work can bring to its students in terms of financial and social capital as well as skills and self-esteem. In this model, work done by young people provides valuable experience and income for the school community (in this case the income does not benefit the child's family directly). Work and school are seen as two key pieces, working together, to enhance the lives of young people. However, the tensions between what we see as good for poor children as opposed to children of privilege remain operative.

The Cristo Rey story has recently been documented by G. R. Kearney, a former volunteer, in *More Than a Dream: How One School's Vision Is Changing the World*.[7] In spite of its far reaching title, the book never shies away from sharing the adversities the school faces, the internal conflicts among faculty and administration, and the struggle to mediate between the real needs of particular children and the cultural assumptions about what is best for them. It is a story with successes, failures, and ongoing compromise.

Cristo Rey Jesuit High School opened 1996 in Pilsen, a neighborhood of Chicago. It was founded by the Chicago Province of the Society of Jesus to serve poor children in the neighborhood who had academic potential but who were without the resources to attend other Catholic schools. To put this criteria in some perspective, Cristo Rey schools generally recruit students who qualify for the federal free or reduced lunch program and who come from families with incomes that are less than 185 percent of the federal poverty level.[8] The schools are in urban neighborhoods and a high percentage of students come from minority populations. One student tells an interviewer, "both of my parents are incarcerated." Students experience violence in their homes and neighborhoods, drug trafficking and gang related crime. Many of their peers in the public school system, whether they are neighbors or siblings, drop out of high school before graduation.[9]

In order to make the school financially viable (a constant challenge), Cristo Rey integrated a corporate internship program into its curriculum.[10] Students would attend school and intern at a business in the Chicago area. Initially this was seen purely as a creative economic solution to the problem of funding the school; it was a matter of paying the bills. The potential educational benefits of this work were not uppermost in the minds of the founders. According to Fr. John Foley, S.J., they simply went to Chicago white collar businesses and said, "Would you give us a job?"[11] This was an important starting point: though the school could rely on only the most nominal tuition fees (if any tuition at all), they did not want to ask for charity in order to sustain the school. They envisioned a very different kind of relationship with the business community—quite unlike the public/private partnerships envisioned by the Reagan administration—one that would give rise to important personal and institutional relationships.

The Chicago business community responded positively and the Corporate Internship Program was born. Students work five days a month at an entry-level position. Essentially, four students share one position by attending school four days each week and staffing the office on the fifth day on a rotating schedule. The company contracts with the school's independently incorporated employment office. The students are technically employees of the internship program, which handles all of their payroll and personnel issues.

The focus is not on individual students working off their personal tuition expenses. Participating corporate sponsors pay the school and not the students. In this way the students work for themselves and for the common good of the school. This is an important distinction. Students are not focused purely on their own advantage and do not compete with others for limited employment opportunities. They support the school together. In addition, Cristo Rey students gain access to working environments that would otherwise be unavailable to them for numerous reasons including basic advantages like transportation and social skills. Students intern in places like financial institutions, law firms, and museums. As one student put it, "we're kids with big people jobs." They benefit from mentoring relationships with their supervisors and coworkers who likewise reap the benefits of working with young people. The students begin to be seen, and to see themselves, as equals.

These are, as we noted earlier, "white collar" positions in environments where advancement requires advancing education. This brings us to another key feature of Cristo Rey schools. Unlike vocational schools that prepare students for work after high school, Cristo Rey schools are explicitly college preparatory institutions grounded in the liberal arts. The goal is for Cristo Rey students to attend college. And they do, in droves. The schools boast a phenomenal college acceptance rate, and an equally envious rate of college attendance, retention, and graduation.[12]

The road for Cristo Rey in Chicago has been a bumpy one. Many of the educators that signed on envisioned a new educational paradigm that could serve poor children by offering them a more creative school environment. A "cutting edge curriculum," however, and its scheduling needs, comes with a price tag, one that is often paid readily in wealthier communities but needs to be justified in poorer ones.[13] Kearney provides a concrete example:

> The minutes from the April 28, 1997, board meeting exhibit growing tension between the academic and financial players on the board. It was becoming clear that they had very different—and often conflicting—approaches to building and managing Cristo Rey.[14]

The faculty and the financial administration saw the "bottom line" from different vantage points. One group was primarily responsible for the balance sheet and the other focused on the change wrought in hearts and minds.[15] The "financial players," board members, and generous donors needed "cost saving ideas" if the school was to remain open and in the black.[16] Other schools serving poor children have less experienced, though no less dedicated, faculty who work for nominal wages or volunteer. Educators wanted the students to have the highest quality education which requires a highly qualified teaching staff. What's more, they wanted the students to be able to ask critical questions about the injustices that perpetuate the cycle of poverty in their neighborhoods.

And while the faculty saw the benefits of the internship program, they raised concerns about its importance relative to academics, noting that, "Cristo Rey students were charged one hundred dollars for missing a day of work. There was no charge for missing class."[17] The perception being that their work, and the income it generated, took precedence over their studies. Kearney notes,

> Nearly 40 percent of the school's income came from foundations—an unprecedented feat in the fundraising world. People liked the idea of students earning their own education. They liked the idea of a school that would be able to support itself, even though at that point it couldn't begin to do so.[18]

The school's new financial model was appealing to supporters, but Kearney's narrative reveals that the model may also have built upon problematic assumptions about what is good for poor children. Business people like youth (presumably poor youth) who work hard and "earn" their education. The common good sees quality education as a basic human right, not something that is earned or a good that children of privilege are entitled to on the assumption that their parents have earned it. We have already encountered in critiques from advocates like Jonathan Kozol, the tendency to think about poor children differently; that is to say that work is good for them. This also places the burden of lifting people out of poverty on the poor themselves. Such a view maintains the imbalance in a charitable relationship: there is a giver and a receiver and the giver controls the terms of the gift. Charitable relationships are necessary but they must be matched by relationships grounded in solidarity.

Mayra Garibay, a Cristo Rey student, put the question most pointedly: "If the Corporate Internship Program is such a good thing, then why don't they have it at St. Ignatius or Loyola Academy?"[19] It would seem that at the more prestigious schools, since they do not require the income, would not benefit from a work/study program. Miss Garibay has already begun to question the roots causes of the injustices that would otherwise keep her from a quality education; and this has lead her even to question the motives of well-meaning supporters. Questions like these and others that the students were raising in the classroom, about racism, for example, had the potential to create unwelcome tensions in their workplaces and among supporters.

The common good perspective that we have outlined calls us to challenge language that suggests education is something to be earned by students who exhibit a certain kind of work ethic. Students do not need to prove themselves worthy of an education. So while we must vigorously maintain that access to education is a basic right of children, it is a right that entails a responsibility. A common good perspective on rights entwines them with responsibilities. Usually, the relationship is framed in this way: the right of *one* entails a duty or an obligation on the part of *another*. So, in the case of education, a child's right becomes the responsibility of the community or the state. If we begin with the experiences at Cristo Rey, another aspect of this relationship emerges. The right to an education also creates responsibility for the rights bearer and her family. Young people, to the extent that they are able (this would be less true for young children), have a responsibility to join in building up the good that is a quality education. Poor children all over the world make tremendous personal sacrifices for a chance to learn to read or calculate. Their burden should be less, and perhaps a sense of obligation should begin to replace a sense of entitlement found among the privileged. In Cristo Rey we see the web of obligations entrusted to families, communities, educators, businesses, and the students themselves in order to the ensure the promise of education.

The students are not passive recipients of the education offered at Cristo Rey. The work they do on behalf of the school gives evidence of that. There are other policies that also build on the sense of students as engaged moral agents. In the words of Fr. Foley, "You want this, come and get it." Attending a Cristo Rey school demands decision on the part of the students. Unlike the market, which promises unlimited choices without real consequences, Cristo Rey recognizes that some choices foreclose others. For example, one particularly challenging policy is the zero tolerance for gang activity. Students are forbidden from "fraternizing" with gang members. Gang involvement is grounds for expulsion as it threatens the safety of the student and the community. For many students, this is a difficult choice especially since it means staying clear of former friends, friends, and even family members. But it is a promise that the students are expected to make and keep with the support of the school.

As Cristo Rey matured and the model taken up in other communities, the work undertaken by the students gained new significance. What started as a strategy to keep a school in Pilsen in the black has blossomed into a hallmark of the Cristo Rey philosophy. The school still communicates to corporate sponsors in a familiar language about a program that is "win-win" in which they gain employees who are dependable, responsible, personable, team players, and self-starters. However, the articulated vision of the meaning of this work has become much richer and has taken on theological import. According to the network's description of the Cristo Rey graduate,

> The graduate has learned the value of work both in the rewards it produces and in the self-satisfaction it allows one to attain. The graduate of Cristo Rey has learned to see work as an invitation to participate in the creative and salvific work of our God as One who labors on our behalf. Work offers the opportunity to discover and demonstrate personal talent—both as stewards and as leaders, and encourages growth. This stewardship implies the responsibility to use all resources wisely for the good of others and the greater glory of God. As a future

leader in the workplace, the Cristo Rey graduate recognizes the dignity of work, its integral connection to justice, and the choices he or she has to create a better society.[20]

Their work becomes a way to share unique gifts and abilities with others in such a way that the fruit of that labor flows to them and to the community. Their work is moral activity that gives glory to God; the work and the relationships to which it gives rise are not mere necessities but genuine goods of social living.

The students at Cristo Rey are crucial to the school's solvency and its success as an academic institution. However, the language we use to describe their activity must be transformed so that the market metaphor loses its stranglehold without denying fiscal realities. The students *are not* "earning" their education; that is their birthright and a claim that they can make against the state and the Christian community. They *are* partnering in making the school and its promises real in the concrete by taking on more responsibility than many other young people. They are stewards, collaborators in the salvific work of building the kingdom, of making God's *shalom* the "status quo."[21]

Working for the kingdom sets Cristo Rey's sights higher than an enviable graduation rate. In the language of Jesuit spirituality, we might call this the "magis" or the "more" that is characteristic of Catholic schools grounded in the Ignatian charism:

> Preparing the students to enter the workforce and be successful was a noble goal and would certainly help some students break the vicious cycle of poverty. But if those students didn't feel compelled to come back to their neighborhood and address the realities that caused the poverty in the first place, what had Cristo Rey really accomplished? Could the school prepare its students to take an active role in effecting change in their community, their city, their country? Could Cristo Rey prepare its graduates to understand the realities of the economic and social structures their parents had encountered and that they, too, would eventually encounter? Could it prepare them to challenge conventional wisdom and ask the difficult questions?[22]

Without aiming for greater social transformation of the social structures that kept their neighborhood in the grips of poverty and its accompanying social ills like gang violence, then Cristo Rey would perpetuate charitable models of social action that maintain unequal power relationships and fail to address root causes of injustice. Alex Molnar has pointed out that many corporations prefer partnerships like these, which bring positive publicity without significant cost, while at the same time they resist changes to a tax structure that could benefit the public schools in neighborhoods like Pilsen. New initiatives in faith-based and private schooling must also be vigorous advocates for public education as a basic human right for which all levels of society, including the business community, bear responsibility. These remains growing edges for initiatives like Cristo Rey and only time will tell if the "more" has been achieved as their graduates make their mark on the world.

What began as one high school serving a poor section of Chicago has since become the Cristo Rey Network with twenty-two schools operating in nineteen states. The Jesuit initiative has welcomed collaborators from a number of other religious orders and dioceses. It is, in the language of the development community, "replicable" and "sustainable." In a recent essay in *America* magazine, Robert Birdsell, president and chief executive officer of the Cristo Rey Network, makes a bid to have faith-based schools like Cristo Rey be welcomed to the table around which U.S. education policy is framed. He notes the role that religious schools, and here Catholic schools stand out for their sheer number, have played in "educating millions of disadvantaged students at no cost to taxpayers." He claims that the Cristo Rey initiative can offer lessons to the broader school system because it has successfully addressed three pressing issues: "providing college preparatory education that accelerates student learning; providing proper preparation for students to enter the workplace; and running schools on a sound financial basis."

Birdsell sees the potential for the Cristo Rey model to be adapted to public secondary schools as well, but only if schools like Cristo Rey have a voice in policy debate. "Faith-based schools are only part of the solution, but as they grow stronger and make this kind of education available to more children in need, they solve a significant portion of the overall problem that many other schools have failed to address."[23]

Kearney concludes his narrative on a realistic note:

> None of these groups had gotten exactly what they wanted as the school was shaped and its policies formed. The school didn't look like what the Jesuits had initially planned. Nor did it look like what the progressive educators had envisioned as a dream school in the inner city. Nor was it the model of efficiency that the businesspeople on the board believed it could be. It was a jumbled mess of compromises.
>
> And that, as much as anything, is why it worked.[24]

Life with children and young people is often a "jumbled mess," "chaos," as Bonnie Miller-McLemore calls it with affection.[25] Like Donald Dunson, Jonathan Kozol, and scores of other committed parents and educators, we are called to take the risk of "entering the chaos" and be ready to take on the arduous and sometimes slow work of building the common good with children.[26]

"We Did It, Ma!"—Alexis, Cristo Rey Alumna

Cristo Rey schools throughout the United States have important lessons to teach as they strive to "get the story straight" both in terms of what real children need to flourish in the concrete and what the gospel demands of us. Not satisfied with educating children of relative privilege, the Jesuits and their collaborators in Pilsen widened their circles of solidarity to include children in this marginalized community. The young people of Pilsen are made in God's image and likeness, claiming compassion and justice. Financial constraints on this endeavor were real and urgent but they were met with imagination and creativity. Having children work is not without complication, as we have seen, and assumptions about how work benefits poor children remain even within the ranks of Cristo Rey supporters. The creativity lies in sharing responsibility with the students for the success of the school as a whole—a success that affords benefits to all participants: students, teachers, administrators, families, the neighborhood, the religious community, and the corporate partners.

We might consider Cristo Rey as Bonnie Miller-McLemore's "pitch in family" writ large. Partnering with the students demands that they be full members of the community, counted among the collaborators in the work of transformation—their own, the community's, and even elements of the workplaces they enter. They are not passive objects of anyone's charity but neither should they be considered exemplars of the individualistic "pull yourself up by your own bootstraps" American myth. The students succeed as part of a community. Perhaps one of the most moving moments in a *60 Minutes* piece on Cristo is when one senior, Alexis, phones her mother to let her know of her acceptance with scholarship money to Xavier University. Her words into the receiver were "We did it, Ma!" One can't help but be struck by the choice of words and the insight that children succeed when there is a "we" in the picture and when young people can count themselves among the "we." Not every student could call home with the same message, but they could all share their joy with the Cristo Rey community.

In the Cristo Rey model, students are agents of the common good of the school and the neighborhood, with greater opportunities for the exercise of agency and authentic human freedom on the horizon. These schools transform the way in which young people can participate in their education and in the market and they open new possibilities for other mediating institutions to live in solidarity with children and young people.

Notes

1. United States Catholic Conference, *Putting Children and Families First: A Challenge for Our Church, Nation and World* (Washington, DC, 1992), 1.

2. Pamela Couture addresses the impact of a number of issues on the well-being of children in *Child Poverty: Love, Justice, and Social Responsibility* (St. Louis, MO: Chalice Press, 2007).

3. I have previously written elsewhere about Cristo Rey, "Children and the Common Good: From Protection to Participation," in *Prophetic Witness: Catholic Women's Strategies for Reform,* ed. Colleen Griffith (New York: Crossroad, 2009), 123–31.

4. Christine E. Gudorf and Regina Wentzel Wolfe, eds., *Ethics and World Religions: Cross Cultural Case Studies* (Maryknoll, NY: Orbis Books, 1999).

5. Cristo Rey Center for the Working Child, Tacna, Peru, barrioperu.terra.com .pe/ccrnt/Ingles/default.htm (accessed November 9, 2006). Jeff Thielman, a former Jesuit international volunteer and current president of North Cambridge Catholic High School, has written with Raymond A. Schroth about his experiences of the center in *Volunteer: With the Poor in Peru* (Bloomington, IN: 1st Books Library, 2000).

6. I was introduced to the Cristo Rey Network by Jeff Thielman, president of North Cambridge Catholic High School, and Margaret Florentine, superintendent of schools for the New Province of the Society of Jesus, in a presentation they gave at the College of the Holy Cross, Worcester, Massachusetts, in September 2005. Margaret Florentine was also generous with resources on the mission of Jesuit secondary education in preparation for this project.

7. G. R. Kearney, *More Than a Dream: How One School's Vision Is Changing the World* (Chicago: Loyola Press, 2008). The Cristo Rey initiative in Chicago has also been highlighted on the television news program *60 Minutes.* Available at www.myncchs .org (accessed May 16, 2009).

8. See www.cristoreynetwork.org/about/FAQ.shtml (accessed May 14, 2009).

9. For testimonials see "One Student at a Time," www.myncchs.org (accessed May 14, 2009).

10. The Corporate Internship Program (CIP) is also referred to as the Hire4Ed Program.

11. *60 Minutes* interview, www.myncchs.org (accessed May 14, 2009).

12. Cristo Rey Network, www.cristoreynetwork.org (accessed May 14, 2009).

13. Kearney, *More Than a Dream,* 243.

14. Kearney, *More Than a Dream,* 181.

15. Kearney, *More Than a Dream,* 220.

16. Kearney, *More Than a Dream,* 182.

17. Kearney, *More Than a Dream,* 212.

18. Kearney, *More Than a Dream,* 214.

19. Kearney, *More Than a Dream,* 319.

20. Cristo Rey Network, www.cristoreynetwork.org (accessed May 14, 2009).

21. Couture, *Child Poverty,* 193.

22. Kearney, *More Than a Dream,* 292.

23. Robert J. Birdsell, "A Catholic Alternative: What's Missing in the Debate on Education," *America* 200, no. 15 (May 11, 2009): 20–21.

24. Kearney, *More Than a Dream,* 369.

25. Bonnie J. Miller-McLemore, *In the Midst of Chaos: Caring for Children as Spiritual Practice* (San Francisco: Jossey-Bass, 2007).

26. Miller-McLemore has also written about moving at the "pace of children" in *Also a Mother: Work and Family as Theological Dilemma* (Nashville, TN: Abingdon Press, 1994). Ethicist James Keenan has written on the virtue of mercy, central to Catholic moral life, and defined it as "entering the chaos of another." See *The Works of Mercy: The Heart of Catholicism* (Lanham, MD: Rowman & Littlefield, 2008).

Conclusion

Keeping Christmas Well

They were a boy and a girl ... Where graceful youth should have filled their features out, and touched them with its freshest tints, a stale and shrivelled hand, like that of age, had pinched, and twisted them, and pulled them into shreds ...

Scrooge started back, appalled. Having them shown to him in this way, he tried to say they were fine children, but the words choked themselves, rather than be parties to a lie of such enormous magnitude.

"Spirit, are they yours?" Scrooge could say no more.

"Have they no refuge or resource?" cried Scrooge.

"Are there no prisons?" said the Spirit, turning on him for the last time with his own words. "Are there no workhouses?"

The bell struck twelve.

—A Christmas Carol, Charles Dickens, 1843

THE GHOSTLY TALE OF EBENEZER SCROOGE is a staple of the Christmas season reminding us that Christmas is a time of giving and thanksgiving that can transform even the most miserly heart. We are repeatedly moved by Tiny Tim, who in spite of his suffering, continues to live in Christmas grace. Some adaptations of the tale are content to convey this message. What may be glossed over, however, are Ignorance and Want, the two children enveloped in the cloak folds of the Spirit of Christmas Present. According to the spirit they are the children of "Man." The waifs are the progeny of stinginess and hard heartedness. Scrooge had contented himself with the taxes he paid and hoarded his wealth without regard to his neighbors in need. Ignorance and

Want are Scrooge's children, humanity's children, our children. In Scrooge's mind, the poor must find resource somewhere, in prisons and workhouses, but surely not in him. Confronted with the consequences of the life he had chosen for himself, Scrooge was horrified and no longer able to be party to the lie that these were "fine children."

A Christmas Carol endures as a classic for many reasons, not the least of which is that the portrait it paints of a particular time in history depicts our contemporary scene as well. The more things change, the more they stay the same. Like the poor in the gospels, Ignorance and Want are still with us and may be joined by another "ugly twin of poverty," the child reared to consume. We see ourselves in Scrooge: "Surely these children must be someone else's responsibility." Poor children are often put to work in inhumane conditions as if a punishment for their poverty or the poverty of their parents.[1] In the United States, child advocate Marian Wright Edelman has decried the "cradle to prison pipeline" that characterizes the prospects for millions of young men of color. Rather than observing a season of joyful anticipation with shared abundance for the poor, our culture falls into the trap that even Ebenezer recognized and resisted, however wrongly: a frantic race to spend and spend in search of happiness only to be met with fleeting pleasure and disappointment. Much of this effort is centered on the children of privilege.

While it may be in the Christmas season that these questions are put before us so starkly, the phenomenon of consumerism is with us all year, year after year, and has global impact. It has become part of the air that we breathe; and we and our children are choking on it.[2] The language and logic of the market has moved steadily into spheres of life beyond the financial sector, including the family and the school. The globalization of Western liberal economic values has had a dramatic impact on the children of the world. The nature of its impact, however, often depends on a child's socioeconomic status. Children of privilege are "little spenders" and "super consumers." They are encouraged to spend and consume with little sense that they can and ought to contribute meaningfully to the welfare of others. Parents seek happiness and advantage for their children and themselves in an atmosphere of competitive consumption without regard to the poverty and environmental devastation it inflicts.

For poor children, the picture can be quite different. In industrialized nations, they are confronted with the same seductive advertising and may experience much of the same disappointment. More often than not, they are considered burdens on the economy, diminishing its ability to maximize wealth for the few. In developing parts of the world, children contribute to family economy and industry through their labor. Millions of children work in inhumane conditions and are denied the opportunities that education affords. They make a tragic choice between school and survival—which is no choice at all. Many children are on their own, a phenomenon worsening in the midst of the HIV and AIDS pandemic.[3] Many children see their work as a valuable contribution to the well-being of their families and communities and as an expression of fidelity in these relationships. Even so, these children long to go to school.

Like the children of other eras, these children have "immense propaganda potential." Rhetoric about their innocence and vulnerability motivates the adult community to act in a spirit of charity which often fails to correct the root causes of injustice. Children deserve our respect, compassion, and solidarity not because they are innocent, or because they are members of families, but because they are human beings made in God's image and likeness. While we may have particular responsibilities to the children in our families, this fact does not mitigate our responsibility to other children. Navigating these obligations and the occasions on which they come into conflict is the task of prudential parenting. It is likewise the task of other organizations and institutions. These must make a preferential option for children, asking how well policies and practices serve the concrete well-being of children, and how well they invite children's presence and participation. Advocating for children does not place one "above" politics, but rather in the very thick of it.

The language of the common good within Christianity provides a fruitful way forward, finding itself at home seated at the table around which we gather to secure the concrete well-being of children. Themes in the common good tradition also find resonance among political theorists arguing from a secular viewpoint and so may open dialogue on practical issues that bridges religious and cultural difference.

In Christian communities, the common good begins with a firm commitment to intrinsic human dignity rooted in the *Imago Dei* and the recognition of our embodied, relational, vulnerable, and transcendent nature. The concept in our time recognizes human rights, including the rights of children, both political and economic, as a meaningful way for society to respond to human dignity. It supports the articulation of children's rights in order to overcome marginalization and make explicit the belief that children are endowed with dignity by a loving God. The common good requires that children have access to our resources. They have a claim on the fruits of our common life.

The theological anthropology which grounds this vision of the common good maintains that children are full, interdependent members of the communities of which they are a part. The common good then also requires that children participate in the building up of the community's resources according to their ability. In the pursuit of the common good the burden of sacrifice, a burden that is inescapable in a fallen world, is shared. It is shared in such a way that no one's basic human flourishing is lost or obscured. Children's well-being is not sacrificed for the collective; rather they take on the responsibility to pursue goods and goals beyond themselves and the benefits of meeting this responsibility flow back to them according to the norms of justice.

Children's participation in the common good is facilitated by several other interlocking themes: the socially transformative family, the principle of subsidiarity, and the preferential option for the poor. Children thrive in families that love them and that have access to the crucial resources needed to nurture children to adulthood. These families themselves are interdependent, requiring access to and support from other social institutions for their well-being. They are called on to contribute to the common good as families. Family life can provide a vital avenue by which children learn and practice solidarity and compassion.

The principle of subsidiarity allows families a certain degree of autonomy in how they provide for their members. Other institutions should not attempt to usurp the family's proper responsibilities. But it also creates an obligation on the part of other organizations to support families in this endeavor and to intervene when families are unable to care for vulnerable members. Subsidiarity provides guidance when the interests of particular children and their families are in conflict. Moreover, the principle respects the competence of grass roots efforts to address the needs of children in particular communities.

The preferential option for poor demands that we measure our practices and policies according to whether and how well they serve the well-being of the poorest among us. Children are often in this category. Poor children have the most urgent claim on our resources. Their needs should form the basis for a community's priorities. Their voices enjoy a privileged place in communal deliberation about how to live together and their experiences are valued sources for moral reasoning.

In the context of consumerism and the prevalence of market values, children's participation in the economic arena is a particularly thorny issue. It does a disservice to children to paint issues like child labor in black and white. The language of rights on its own, or the language of traditional family values may not be able to chart a course through the immense gray. The language of the common good can help us in the midst of such complexity. We can challenge the inhumane work done by children and the intense, intrusive forms of marketing that have become commonplace, both of which are distortions of a commitment to human dignity and freedom. At the same time, those who pursue the common good can join in solidarity with children who work, acknowledge the support they give to their families, honor their commitment to family obligations, and strive with them to secure access to other basic goods and services like education, health care, and recreation. And, we can begin to ask more of children of privilege. We can honor their unique gifts and abilities, resist the temptation to see children as a mark of status, redirect our desires for the "perfect child" in order to insure the basic well-being of other people's children, and resist the drive to gain advantage over others through consumption.

There are children and families who bear witness to the claims of the common good. They are the new icons of childhood and family: transformed by the good news of the gospel and transforming the world around them. The children of the world need for all institutions of society to play a part in supporting local efforts and in elevating the conversation to the highest levels of organization and action. We have seen one such attempt in the U.S. educational context. Initiatives like the Cristo Rey Network of schools not only seek the well-being of poor children by offering a quality education that calls forth each child's gifts but the network also recognizes the students as partners in this endeavor without whom the project fails.

Cristo Rey schools are committed to the intrinsic dignity of their students and have chosen to place their competence, energy, and fidelity at the service of poor children. Through their internship programs, the students not only advance their own interests, but participate in building the common good of the community as well. They are valued collaborators in making the promises of education real in the concrete. Their work has theological significance—this is the work of the kingdom. Meeting these obligations enhances rather than limits the students' exercise of human freedom. The same cannot be said of the dehumanizing labor undertaken by millions of the world's children. Beyond this, the network has created concrete opportunities for other agents in the profit and not-for-profit sectors to be in solidarity with young people. Finally, the Cristo Rey model has been adapted to the needs of twenty-two (and counting) local communities who enjoy the benefits of being part of a larger network—subsidiarity in action. Creative initiatives like Cristo Rey should be encouraged and fostered by individuals, families, religious communities, corporations, philanthropic organizations, governments, and other institutions.

The passage from Isaiah with which we began this exploration is indeed a vision of the common good for all creation, one in which children thrive and play, and yes, lead. For Christians, the birth of a vulnerable infant in meager surroundings and stalked by the fear of a tyrant signals the in-breaking of God's kingdom in human history. It is far from an ideal beginning and yet Christians believe that this is the little child who would lead us in the path of salvation. Those who draw near and live, as Margaret Eletta Guider says, "in the shadow of the manger," glimpse the promise of God's *shalom*. Like the magi, they are forever changed and must go home by another route in order to remain true to what they have seen and heard.[4] For those who pursue the common good this route is a bumpy, winding road traveled in solidarity with the children of the world.

Notes

1. Cristina Traina, "For the Sins of the Parents: Roman Catholic Ethics and the Politics of Family," in *Prophetic Witness: Women's Strategies for Reform*, ed. Colleen Griffith (New York: Crossroad, 2009), 114–22.

2. This image is used powerfully by Margaret Farley in *Compassionate Respect: A Feminist Approach to Medical Ethics and Other Questions* (Mahwah, NJ: Paulist Press, 2003), in reference to sexism.

3. Mary M. Doyle Roche, "Children and the Common Good," in *Calling for Justice throughout the World: Catholic Women Theologians on the HIV/AIDS Pandemic*, ed. Mary Jo Iozzio, Elsie Miranda, and Mary M. Doyle Roche (New York: Continuum, 2009), 127–33.

4. Margaret Eletta Guider, "Living in the Shadow of the Manger: Mission, Ecumenism, and the State of the World's Children," *Word and World* 18, no. 2 (Spring 1998): 179–86.

Bibliography

Acuff, Dan S., with Robert H. Reiher. *What Kids Buy and Why: The Psychology of Marketing to Kids.* New York: The Free Press, 1997.

Adatto, Kiku. "Selling Out Childhood." *The Hedgehog Review* 5, no. 2 (Summer 2003): 24–40.

Albrecht, Gloria H. *Hitting Home: Feminist Ethics, Women's Work, and the Betrayal of Family Values.* New York: Continuum, 2002.

Anderson, Herbert, and Susan B. W. Johnson. *Regarding Children: A New Respect for Childhood and Families.* Louisville, KY: Westminster John Knox Press, 1994.

———. "A Sanctuary for Childhood in a Culture of Indifference." *Word and World* 15, no. 1 (Winter 1995): 32–29.

Andolsen, Barbara Hilkert, Christine E. Gudorf, Mary D. Pellauer, eds. *Women's Consciousness, Women's Conscience: A Reader in Feminist Ethics.* San Francisco: Harper and Row, 1985.

Annan, Kofi. "We the Children." *Secretary General's Report to the United Nations.* June 2001.

Ariès, Philippe. *L'Enfant et la vie familiale sous l'ancien regime.* Paris: Libraire Plon, 1960. Translated by Robert Baldick as *Centuries of Childhood: A Social History of Family Life.* New York: Alfred A. Knopf, 1962.

Bakke, O. M. *When Children Became People: The Birth of Childhood in Early Christianity.* Minneapolis: Fortress Press, 2005.

Barton, Stephen C. *Discipleship and Family Ties in Mark and Matthew.* Cambridge: Cambridge University Press, 1994.

———, ed. *The Family in Theological Perspective.* Edinburgh: T&T Clark, 1996.

———. "Jesus—Friend of Little Children?" In *Contours of Christian Education,* edited by Jeff Astley and David Day, 30–40. Great Wakering, UK: McCrimmons, 1992.

Beaudoin, Tom. *Consuming Faith: Integrating Who We Are with What We Buy.* Lanham, MD: Sheed & Ward, 2003.

Beder, Sharon. *Selling the Work Ethic: From Puritan Pulpit to Corporate PR.* London and New York: Zed Books, 2000.

Benedict XV. *Annus iam plenus* (December 1, 1919). In *The Papal Encyclicals*, vol. 3, *1903–1939*, compiled by Claudia Carlen, 170. Wilmington, NC: McGrath, 1981.

Birdsell, Robert J. "A Catholic Alternative: What's Missing in the Debate on Education." *America* 200, no. 15 (May 11, 2009): 20–21.

Boston College Church in the Twenty-first Century Initiative. *C21 Resources.* Spring 2003.

Boswell, John. *The Kindness of Strangers: The Abandonment of Children in Western Europe from Late Antiquity to the Renaissance.* New York: Pantheon Books, 1988.

Bourg, Florence Caffrey. *Where Two or Three Are Gathered: Christian Families as Domestic Churches.* Notre Dame, IN: University of Notre Dame Press, 2004.

Brennan, Patrick McKinley, ed. *The Vocation of the Child.* Grand Rapids, MI: Eerdmans, 2008.

Browning, Don S. *Equality and the Family: A Fundamental Practical Theology of Children, Mothers, and Fathers in Modern Society.* Grand Rapids, MI: Eerdmans, 2007.

———. "Should the UN Convention on the Rights of the Child Be Ratified and Why?" Paper delivered at the Annual Meeting of the American Academy of Religion, 2006.

Browning, Don S., and Ian Evison. "The Family Debate: A Middle Way." *The Christian Century*, July 14–21, 1993, 712–16.

Browning, Don S., and Bonnie J. Miller-McLemore, eds. *Children and Childhood in American Religions.* Camden, NJ: Rutgers University Press, 2009.

Browning, Don S., Bonnie J. Miller-McLemore, Pamela D. Couture, K. Brynolf Lyon, and Robert M. Franklin, eds. *From Culture Wars to Common Ground: Religion and the American Family Debate.* Louisville, KY: Westminster John Knox Press, 1997.

Brubaker, Pamela K., Rebecca Todd Peters, and Laura A. Stivers, eds. *Justice in a Global Economy.* Louisville, KY: Westminster John Knox, 2006.

Brueggemann, Walter. "Will Our Faith Have Children?" *Word and World* 3, no. 3 (1983): 272–83.

Bryk, Anthony S., Valerie E. Lee, and Peter B. Holland. *Catholic Schools and the Common Good.* Cambridge, MA: Harvard University Press, 1993.

Bunge, Marcia J., ed. *The Child in Christian Thought.* Grand Rapids, MI: Eerdmans, 2001.

Bunge, Marcia J., with Terrence E. Fretheim and Beverly Roberts Gaventa. *The Child in the Bible.* Grand Rapids, MI: Eerdmans, 2008.

Burggraeve, Roger. "From Responsible to Meaningful Sexuality: An Ethics of Growth as an Ethics of Mercy for Young People in This Era of AIDS." In *Catholic Ethicists on HIV/AIDS Prevention,* edited by James F. Keenan, Jon Fuller, Lisa Sowle Cahill, and Kevin Kelly, 303–16. New York: Continuum, 2000.

Cahill, Lisa Sowle. *Family: A Christian Social Perspective.* Minneapolis: Fortress Press, 2000.

———. "Marriage: Developments in Catholic Theology and Ethics." *Theological Studies* 64, no. 1 (March 2003): 78–105.

Camacho, Agnes Zenaida V. "Family, Child Labour and Migration: Child Domestic Workers in Metro Manila." *Childhood* 6, no. 1 (1999): 57–73.

Campbell, David. "Making Democratic Education Work: Schools, Social Capital, and Civic Education." Paper presented at the Conference on Charter Schools, Vouchers, and Public Education, March 2000.

Capps, Randy, Rosa Maria Castañeda, Ajay Chaudry, and Robert Santos. *Paying the Price: The Impact of Immigration Raids on America's Children.* Washington, DC: National Council of La Raza, 2007.

Carr, Anne, and Mary Stewart van Leeuwen, eds. *Religion, Feminism, and the Family.* Louisville, KY: Westminster John Knox Press, 1996.

Children's Defense Fund. *Wasting America's Future: The Children's Defense Fund's Report on the Costs of Child Poverty.* Boston: Beacon Press, 1994.

Cimino, Carol, Regina M. Haney, and Joseph M. O'Keefe, eds. *Integrating the Social Teaching of the Church into Catholic Schools: Conversations in Excellence 2000.* Washington, DC: National Catholic Education Association, 2001.

Coffey, Tim, David Siegel, and Greg Livingston. *Mom and Kid: Marketing to the New Super Consumer.* Ithaca, NY: Paramount Market Publishing, 2006.

Coles, Robert. *Children of Crisis: A Study of Courage and Fear.* Boston and Toronto: Little, Brown and Co., 1967.

———. *The Moral Intelligence of Children: How to Raise a Moral Child.* New York: Plume 1997.

———. "Struggling toward Childhood: An Interview with Robert Coles." *Second Opinion* 18, no. 4 (April 1993): 58–71.

Cooey, Paula M. "That Every Child Who Wants Might Learn to Dance." *Cross Currents* 48, no. 2 (Summer 1998): 185–97.

Coontz, Stephanie. *The Way We Never Were: American Families and the Nostalgia Trap.* New York: Basic Books, 2000.

———. *The Way We Really Are: Coming to Terms with America's Changing Families.* New York: Basic Books, 1997.

Couture, Pamela D. *Blessed Are the Poor? Women's Poverty, Family Policy and Practical Theology.* Nashville, TN: Abingdon Press, 1991.

———. *Child Poverty: Love, Justice, and Social Responsibility.* St. Louis, MO: Chalice Press, 2007.

———. *Seeing Children, Seeing God: A Practical Theology of Children and Poverty.* Nashville, TN: Abingdon Press, 2000.

Crane, Valerie, and Milton Chen. "Content Development of Children's Media." In *The Faces of Televisual Media: Teaching, Violence, Selling to Children,* edited by Edward L. Palmer and Brian M. Young, 55–81. Mahwah, NJ: Lawrence Erlbaum Associates, 2003.

Cunningham, Hugh. *Children and Childhood in Western Society Since 1500.* London and New York: Longman, 1995.

———. *The Children of the Poor: Representations of Childhood Since the 17th Century.* Oxford and Cambridge, MA: Blackwell, 1991.

———. "Histories of Childhood." *American Historical Review,* October 1988, 1195–208.

———. "The History of Childhood." In *Images of Childhood,* edited by C. Philip Hwang, Michael E. Lamb, and Irving E. Sigel, 27–35. Mahwah, NJ: Lawrence Erlbaum Associates, 1996.

Curren, Charles, Margaret A. Farley, and Richard A. McCormick, eds. *Feminist Ethics and the Catholic Moral Tradition.* New York: Paulist Press, 1996.

De Cea-Naharro, Maragrita Pintos. "Women's Right to Full Citizenship and Decision-Making in the Church." *Concilium*, May 2002, 79–87.

DeCrane, Susanne M. *Aquinas, Feminism, and the Common Good.* Washington, DC: Georgetown University Press, 2004.

Dialog 37. Summer 1998.

Dixon, Suzanne. "The Sentimental Ideal of the Roman Family." In *Marriage, Divorce, and Children in Ancient Rome*, edited by Beryl Rawson, 99–113. Oxford: Clarendon Press, 1991.

Dunson, Donald. *Child, Victim, Soldier: The Loss of Innocence in Uganda.* Maryknoll, NY: Orbis, 2008.

———. "The Child Soldiers of Gusco." *America* 186, no. 2 (January 21–28, 2002): 12–16.

———. *No Room at the Table: Earth's Most Vulnerable Children.* Maryknoll, NY: Orbis, 2003.

Dwyer, Judith, ed. *New Dictionary of Catholic Social Thought.* Collegeville, MN: Liturgical Press, 1994.

Edelman, Marian Wright. "The Children We Have in Trust." *Sojourner's Magazine*, April 1994, 17.

———. *The Measure of Our Success: A Letter to My Children and Yours.* Boston: Beacon Press, 1992.

———. *The Sea Is So Wide and My Boat Is So Small: Charting a Course for the Next Generation.* New York: Hyperion, 2008.

Elshtain, Jean Bethke. "Family Matters: The Plight of America's Children." *The Christian Century*, July 14–21, 1993, 710–12.

Farley, Margaret A. "The Church and the Family: An Ethical Task." *Horizons* 10, no. 1 (1983): 50–71.

———. *Compassionate Respect: A Feminist Approach to Medical Ethics and Other Questions.* Madeleva Lecture. Mahwah, NJ: Paulist Press, 2003.

Farmer, Paul. *Pathologies of Power: Health, Human Rights and the New War on the Poor.* Berkeley: University of California Press, 2003.

Fernando, Jude L. "Children's Rights: Beyond the Impasse." *The Annals of the American Academy of Political and Social Science* 575, no. 1 (2001): 8–24.

Fewell, Danna Nolan. *The Children of Israel: Reading the Bible for the Sake of Our Children.* Nashville, TN: Abingdon Press, 2003.

Francis, James. "Children and Childhood in the New Testament." In *Family in Theological Perspective*, edited by Stephen C. Barton, 65–85. Edinburgh: T&T Clark, 1996.

———. "Childhood and Jesus." *Priests and People* 15, no. 12 (December 2001).

Frederiksen, Lisa. "Child and Youth Employment in Denmark: Comments on Children's Work from Their Own Perspective." *Children* 6, no. 1 (1999): 101–12.

Grace, Gerald. *Catholic Schools: Mission, Markets and Morality.* London and New York: Routledge Falmer, 2002.

Grace, Gerald, and Joseph O'Keefe. "Catholic Schools Facing the Challenges of the 21st Century: An Overview." In *International Handbook of Catholic Education:*

Challenges for School Systems in the 21st Century, Part I, edited by Gerald Grace and Joseph O'Keefe, 1–11. Dordrecht: The Netherlands, 2007.

———, eds. *International Handbook of Catholic Education: Challenges for School Systems in the 21st Century, Part I.* Dordrecht, The Netherlands: Springer, 2007.

Greven, Philip. *Spare the Child: The Religious Roots of Punishment and the Psychological Impact of Physical Abuse.* New York: Alfred A. Knopf, 1991.

Groome, Thomas H. "What Makes a School Catholic?" In *The Contemporary Catholic School: Context, Identity and Diversity,* edited by Terence H. McLaughlin, Joseph O'Keefe, and Bernadette O'Keeffe. London and Washington, DC: The Falmer Press, 1996.

Gudorf, Christine E. "Dissecting Parenthood: Infertility, in Vitro, and Other Lessons in Why and How We Parent." *Conscience* 15, no. 3 (Autumn 1994): 15–22.

———. "Parenting, Mutual Love and Sacrifice." In *Women's Consciousness, Women's Conscience: A Reader in Feminist Ethics,* edited by Barbara Hilkert Andolsen, Christine E. Gudorf, and Mary D. Pellauer, 175–91. San Francisco: Harper and Row, 1985.

———. "Rights of Children." In *The New Dictionary of Catholic Social Thought,* edited by Judith Dwyer, 143–48. Collegeville, MN: Liturgical Press, 1994.

———. "Sacrifice and Parental Spiritualities." In *Religion, Feminism, and the Family,* edited by Anne Carr and Mary Stewart van Leeuwen, 294–309. Louisville, KY: Westminster John Knox Press, 1996.

———. *Victimization: Examining Christian Complicity.* Philadelphia: Trinity Press International, 1992.

———. "Western Religion and the Patriarchal Family." In *Feminist Ethics and the Catholic Moral Tradition,* edited by Charles E. Curran, Margaret E. Farley, and Richard McCormick, 251–77. Mahwah, NJ: Paulist Press, 1996.

Gudorf, Christine E., and Regina Wentzel Wolfe, eds. *Ethics and World Religions: Cross Cultural Case Studies.* Maryknoll, NY: Orbis Books, 1999.

Guggenheim, Martin. *What's Wrong with Children's Rights?* Cambridge, MA: Harvard University Press, 2005.

Guider, Margaret Eletta. "Children and Mission." In *Dictionary of Mission: Theology, History, Perspectives,* edited by Karl Müller, Theo Sundermeier, Stephen B. Bevans, and Richard H. Bliese, 53–55. Maryknoll, NY: Orbis, 1997.

———. "Living in the Shadow of the Manger: Mission, Ecumenism, and the State of the World's Children." *Word and World* 18, no. 2 (Spring 1998): 179–86.

Gundry-Volf, Judith M. "The Least and the Greatest: Children in the New Testament." In *The Child in Christian Thought,* edited by Marcia J. Bunge, 29–60. Grand Rapids, MI: Eerdmans, 2001.

Gunter, Barrie, Caroline Oates, and Mark Blades. *Advertising to Children on TV: Content, Impact, and Regulation.* Mahwah, NJ: Lawrence Erlbaum Associates, 2005.

Guy, Kathleen A. *Welcome the Child: A Child Advocacy Guide for Churches.* Washington, DC: Children's Defense Fund, 1991.

Hafen, Bruce C., and Jonathan O. Hafen. "Abandoning Children to Their Rights." *First Things,* August/September 1995, 18–24.

Halberstam, David. *The Children.* New York: Random House, 1998.

Haney, Regina, and Joseph O'Keefe, eds. *Conversations in Excellence: Providing for the Diverse Needs of Youth and Their Families*. Washington, DC: National Catholic Education Association, 1998.

Hauerwas, Stanley. *A Community of Character: Toward a Constructive Christian Social Ethic*. Notre Dame, IN: University of Notre Dame Press, 1981.

Hawes, Joseph, M. *The Children's Rights Movement: A History of Advocacy and Protection*. Boston: Twayne Publishers, 1991.

Hazelton, Angela. "Protecting Our Children." *Priests and People* 15, no. 12 (December 2001): 452–55.

Heller, Scott. "The Meaning of Children Becomes a Focal Point of Scholars." *Chronicle of Higher Education* 7 (August 1998): A14–16.

Hennelly, Alfred T., ed. *Liberation Theology: A Documentary History*. Maryknoll, NY: Orbis Books, 1990.

Hennelly, Alfred T., and John Langan, eds. *Human Rights in the Americas: The Struggle for Consensus*. Washington, DC: Georgetown University Press, 1982.

Herzog, Kristin. *Children and Our Global Future*. Cleveland: Pilgrim Press, 2005.

Heywood, Colin. *A History of Childhood: Children and Childhood in the West from Medieval to Modern Times*. Cambridge: Polity, 2001.

Himes, Kenneth R. "Consumerism and Christian Ethics." *Theological Studies* 68 (2007): 132–53.

Hindman, Hugh D. *Child Labor: An American History*. Armonk, NY: M. E. Sharpe, 2002.

Hinsdale, Mary Ann. "'Infinite Openness to the Infinite': Karl Rahner's Contribution to Modern Catholic Thought on the Child." In *The Child in Christian Thought*, edited by Marcia J. Bunge, 406–45. Grand Rapids, MI: Eerdmans, 2001.

Hinze, Christine Firer. "John A. Ryan, Public Policy, and the Quest for a Dignified Ecology of Work." In *Religion and Public Life: The Legacy of Monsignor John A. Ryan*, edited by Robert G. Kennedy et al. Lanham, MD: University Press of America, 2001.

Hochschild, Arlie Russell. *The Time Bind: When Work Becomes Home and Home Becomes Work*. New York: Henry Holt and Co., 1997.

Hochschild, Arlie Russell, and Anne Machung. *The Second Shift*. New York: Avon Books, 1990.

Hollenbach, David. *The Common Good and Christian Ethics*. Cambridge: Cambridge University Press, 2002.

———. "The Common Good, Pluralism and Catholic Education." In *The Contemporary Catholic School: Context, Identity and Diversity*, edited by Terence McLaughlin, Joseph O'Keefe, and Bernadette O'Keeffe, 89–103. London: Falmer Press, 1996.

Hwang, C. Philip, Michael E. Lamb, and Irving E. Sigel, eds. *Images of Childhood*. Mahwah, NJ: Lawrence Erlbaum Associates, 1996.

Hymowitz, Kay S. "The Contradictions of Parenting in a Media Age." In *Kid Stuff: Marketing Sex and Violence to America's Children*, edited by Diane Ravitch and Joseph P. Viteritti, 214–39. Baltimore: Johns Hopkins University Press, 2003.

Interpretation: A Journal of Bible and Theology 55, no. 2 (April 2001).

Jacoby, Jeff. "Separating School and State." *Boston Globe*, June 12, 2005, D11.

Jensen, David H. *Graced Vulnerability: A Theology of Childhood*. Cleveland: Pilgrim Press, 2005.

John Paul II. *Familiaris Consortio.* Washington, DC: United States Conference of Catholic Bishops, 1982.

John XXIII. *Mater et Magistra (Christianity and Social Progress).* Papal encyclical, 1961.

Johnson, Maxwell E. *Living Water, Sealing Spirit: Readings on Christian Initiation.* Collegeville, MN: Liturgical Press, 1995.

Junker-Kenny, Maureen, and Norbert Mette, eds. *Little Children Suffer.* Maryknoll, NY: Orbis Books, 1996.

Kearney, G. R. *More Than a Dream: How One School's Vision Is Changing the World.* Chicago: Loyola Press, 2008.

Keenan, James F. *Virtues for Ordinary Christians.* Lanham, MD: Sheed & Ward, 1996.

———. *The Works of Mercy: The Heart of Catholicism.* Lanham, MD: Rowman & Littlefield, 2008.

Keenan, James F., and Jon D. Fuller. "The International AIDS Conference in Bangkok: Two Views." *America* 191, no. 5 (August 30–September 6, 2004): 13–16.

———. "The Language of Human Rights and Social Justice in the Face of HIV/AIDS." *BUDHI* 1 & 2 (2004): 211–31.

Keenan, James F., Jon D. Fuller, Lisa Sowle Cahill, and Kevin Kelly, eds. *Catholic Ethicists on HIV/AIDS Prevention.* New York: Continuum, 2000.

Kennedy, David. "The Hermeneutics of Childhood." *Philosophy Today* 36 (Spring 1992): 44–58.

Kielburger, Craig, with Kevin Major. *Free the Children: A Young Man Fights Against Child Labor and Proves That Children Can Change the World.* New York: Harper Perennial, 2000.

King, Wilma. *African American Childhoods: Historical Perspectives from Slavery to Civil Rights.* New York: Palgrave/Macmillan, 2005.

Kozol, Jonathan. *Ordinary Resurrections: Children in the Years of Hope.* New York: Crown Publishers, 2000.

———. *Savage Inequalities: Children in America's Schools.* New York: Harper Perennial, 1992.

Lakshmanan, Indira A. R. "In Danger's Way: Trapped in Cycles of Poverty, Children Toil in Bolivia's Mines." *Boston Globe* June 26, 2005, A1, A10.

Lawler, Michael G. *Family: American and Christian.* Chicago: Loyola Press, 1998.

Leach, Penelope. *Children First: What Society Must Do—and Is Not Doing—for Children Today.* New York: Alfred A Knopf, 1994.

Lewis, Barbara A. *A Kid's Guide to Social Action.* Minneapolis, MN: Free Spirit Publishing, 1998.

Lindstrom, Martin, with Patricia B. Seybold. *Brand Child: Remarkable Insights into the Minds of Today's Global Kids and Their Relationships with Brands.* London: Kogan Page, 2004.

Linn, Susan. *Consuming Kids: The Hostile Takeover of Childhood.* New York: The New Press, 2004.

Living Pulpit: The Child 12, no. 4 (October–December 2003).

Majib, Sabita. "Watch Out . . ." *The Hindu Business Line,* June 10, 2005. www.thehindu businessline.com.

Martinson, Floyd M. *The Sexual Life of Children.* Westport, CT, and London: Bergin and Garvey, 1994.

Marty, Martin E. *The Mystery of the Child.* Grand Rapids, MI: Eerdmans, 2007.

Maryknoll, September 2001.

Massaro, Thomas. *Catholic Social Teaching and United States Welfare Reform.* Collegeville, MN: Liturgical Press, 1998.

———. *Living Justice: Catholic Social Teaching in Action.* Lanham, MD: Sheed & Ward, 2000.

Matthews, Gareth. *Philosophy and the Young Child.* Cambridge, MA: Harvard University Press, 1980.

———. *The Philosophy of Childhood.* Cambridge, MA: Harvard University Press, 1994.

Matthews, Gareth, and Robert Coles. *Dialogues with Children.* Cambridge, MA: Harvard University Press, 1992.

Mayor, Tracy. "What Are Video Games Turning Us Into?" *Boston Globe Magazine,* February 20, 2005, 18–21, 32–37.

McCarthy, David Matzko. *The Good Life: Genuine Christianity for the Middle Class.* Grand Rapids, MI: Brazos Press, 2004.

McCormick, Patrick T. "Fit to Be Tried?" *America* 186, no. 4 (February 11, 2002): 15–18.

McDonough, Mary J. *Can a Health Care Market Be Moral? A Catholic Vision.* Washington, DC: Georgetown University Press, 2007.

McGinnis, J. Michael, Jennifer Gootman, and Vivica I. Kraak, eds. *Food Marketing to Children and Youth: Threat or Opportunity?* Washington, DC: National Academies Press, 2006.

McKechnie, Jim, and Sandy Hobbs. "Child Labour: The View from the North." *Childhood* 6, no. 1 (1999): 89–100.

McLaughlin, Terence H., Joseph O'Keefe, and Bernadette O'Keeffe, eds. *The Contemporary Catholic School: Context, Identity and Diversity.* London and Washington, DC: The Falmer Press, 1996.

McNeal, James U. *Kids as Customers: A Handbook of Marketing to Children.* New York: Lexington Books, 1992.

———. *The Kids Market: Myths and Realities.* Ithaca, NY: Paramount Market Publishing, 1999.

Mercer, Joyce Ann. *Welcoming Children: A Practical Theology of Childhood.* St. Louis, MO: Chalice Press, 2005.

Messer, Donald E. *Breaking the Conspiracy of Silence, Christian Churches and the Global AIDS Crisis.* Minneapolis: Fortress Press, 2004.

Meyers, William E. "Considering Child Labour: Changing Terms, Issues and Actors at the International Level." *Childhood* 6, no. 1 (1999): 13–26.

———. "The Right Rights? Child Labor in a Globalizing World." *The Annals of the American Academy of Political and Social Science* 575, no. 1 (2001): 38–55.

Miljeteig, Per. "Children's Participation: Giving Children the Opportunity to Develop into Active and Responsible Members of Society." *Social Education* 56, no. 4 (April 1992): 216.

———. "Creating Partnerships with Working Children and Youth." *Social Protection Discussion Paper Series,* no. 0021. Washington, DC: Human Development Network, The World Bank, 2000.

Miller, Richard B. *Children, Ethics, and Modern Medicine.* Bloomington and Indianapolis: University of Indiana Press, 2003.

Miller-McLemore, Bonnie J. *Also a Mother: Work and Family as Theological Dilemma.* Nashville, TN: Abingdon Press, 1994.

———. *In the Midst of Chaos: Caring for Children as Spiritual Practice.* San Francisco: Jossey-Bass, 2007.

———. "Let the Children Come." *Second Opinion* 17, no. 1 (July 1991): 10–25.

———. *Let the Children Come: Reimagining Childhood from a Christian Perspective.* San Francisco: Jossey-Bass, 2003.

Molnar, Alex. *Giving Kids the Business: The Commercialization of America's Schools.* Boulder, CO: Westview Press, 1996.

Müller, Karl, Theo Sundermeier, Stephen B. Bevans, and Richard H. Bliese, eds. *Dictionary of Mission: Theology, History, Perspectives.* Maryknoll, NY: Orbis Books, 1997.

O'Brien, David J., and Thomas A. Shannon, eds. *Catholic Social Thought: The Documentary Heritage.* Maryknoll, NY: Orbis Books, 1992.

O'Connell Davidson, Julia. *Children in the Global Sex Trade.* Cambridge: Polity Press, 2005.

O'Keefe, Joseph, M. "Children and Community Service: Character Education in Action." *Journal of Education* 179, no. 2 (1997): 47–62.

———. "No Margin, No Mission." In *The Contemporary Catholic School: Context, Identity and Diversity,* edited by Terence H. McLaughlin, Joseph O'Keefe, and Bernadette O'Keeffe, 177–97. London and Washington, DC: Falmer Press, 1996.

———. "Values and Identity in Catholic Education: A Response to Rabbi Michael A. Paley." *Catholic Education: A Journal of Theory and Practice* 1, no. 3 (March 1998): 322–33.

Okin, Susan Moller. *Justice, Gender and the Family.* New York: Basic Books, 1989.

Osiek, Carolyn. "The Family in Early Christianity: 'Family Values' Revisited." *Catholic Biblical Quarterly* 58, no. 1 (January 1996): 1–24.

Ozment, Stephen. *When Fathers Ruled: Family Life in Reformation Europe.* Cambridge, MA: Harvard University Press, 1983.

Paley, Vivian Gussin. *The Kindness of Children.* Cambridge, MA: Harvard University Press, 1999.

Palmer, Edward L., and Brian M. Young, eds. *The Faces of Televisual Media: Teaching, Violence, Selling to Children.* Mahwah, NJ: Lawrence Erlbaum Associates, 2003.

Pattison, Robert. *The Child Figure in English Literature.* Athens: University of Georgia Press, 1978.

Peters, Ted. *For the Love of Children: Genetic Technology and the Future of the Family.* Louisville, KY: Westminster John Knox Press, 1996.

Piaget, Jean. *The Child's Conception of the World.* London: Kegan Paul, 1929.

———. *The Moral Judgment of the Child.* Reprint, New York: Free Press, 1965.

Pope, Stephen J. *Human Evolution and Christian Ethics.* Cambridge: Cambridge University Press, 2007.

Post, Stephen G. *More Lasting Unions: Christianity, the Family and Society.* Grand Rapids, MI: Eerdmans, 2000.

———. *Spheres of Love: Toward a New Ethics of the Family.* Dallas: Southern Methodist University Press, 1994.

Priests and People 15, no. 12 (December 2001).

Putnam, Robert D. *Bowling Alone: The Collapse and Revival of American Community.* New York: Simon & Schuster, 2000.

Rahner, Karl. "Ideas for a Theology of Childhood." *Theological Investigations,* vol. 8. New York: Seabury Press, 1977.

Ravitch, Diane, and Joseph P. Viteritti, eds. *Kid Stuff: Marketing Sex and Violence to America's Children.* Baltimore: Johns Hopkins University Press, 2003.

Rawson, Beryl, ed. *The Family in Ancient Rome: New Perspectives.* Ithaca, NY: Cornell University Press, 1986.

———. *Marriage, Divorce, and Children in Ancient Rome.* Oxford: Clarendon Press, 1991.

Roberts-Davis, Tanya. *We Need to Go to School: Voices of the Rugmark Children.* Toronto: Groundwood, 2001.

Roche, Mary M. Doyle. "Children and the Common Good." In *Calling for Justice throughout the World: Catholic Women Theologians on the HIV/AIDS Pandemic,* edited by Mary Jo Iozzio, Mary M. Doyle Roche, and Elsie Miranda, 127–33. New York: Continuum, 2009.

———. "Children and the Common Good: From Protection to Participation." In *Prophetic Witness: Catholic Women's Strategies for Reform,* edited by Colleen Griffith, 123–31. New York: Crossroad, 2009.

———. "A Little Child Will Lead Them." *Living Pulpit* 12, no. 4 (October–December 2003): 14–15.

Rogerson, John. "The Family and Structures of Grace in the Old Testament." In *Family in Theological Perspective,* edited by Stephen C. Barton, 25–42. Edinburgh: T&T Clark, 1996.

Ross, Lainie Friedman. *Children, Families, and Health Care Decision-Making.* Oxford: Clarendon Press, 1998.

Rubio, Julie Hanlon. *A Christian Theology of Marriage and Family.* New York and Mahwah, NJ: Paulist Press, 2003.

———. "Does Family Conflict with Community?" *Theological Studies* 58, no. 4 (December 1997): 597–617.

———. "Dual Vocation of Christian Parents." *Theological Studies* 63, no. 4 (December 2002): 786–812.

———. "Three-in-One Flesh: A Christian Reappraisal of Divorce in Light of Recent Studies." *Journal of the Society of Christian Ethics* 23, no. 1 (Spring–Summer 2003): 47–70.

———. "Toward a Theology of Children: Questions from an Emerging Field of Inquiry." *INTAMS Review* 9, no. 2 (Autumn 2003): 188–99.

Ryan, Maura A. *Ethics and Economics of Assisted Reproduction: The Cost of Longing.* Washington, DC: Georgetown University Press, 2001.

Sanders, David. "A Space for Growth." *Priests and People* 15, no. 12 (December 2001): 438.

Schor, Juliet B. "America's Most Wanted." *Boston College Magazine* 64, no. 4 (Fall 2004): 30–37.

———. *Born to Buy: The Commercialized Child and the New Consumer Culture.* New York: Scribner, 2004.

———. "The Commodification of Childhood: Tales from the Advertising Front Lines." *The Hedgehog Review* 5, no. 2 (Summer 2003): 7–23.

———. "Work, Family and Children's Consumer Culture." www2.bc.edu/~schorj/ConsumerCulture.pdf.

Schüssler Fiorenza, Elisabeth. *In Memory of Her: A Feminist Reconstruction of Christian Origins, Tenth Anniversary Edition.* New York: Crossroad, 1995.

Searle, Mark. "Infant Baptism Reconsidered." In *Living Water, Sealing Spirit: Readings on Christian Initiation,* edited by Maxwell E. Johnson, 365–409. Collegeville, MN: Liturgical Press, 1995.

Shahar, Shulamith. *Childhood in the Middle Ages.* London: Routledge, 1990.

Singer, P. W. "Caution: Children at War." *Parameters: U.S. Army War College Quarterly* 31, no. 4 (Winter 2001–2002): 40–56.

Slawson, Douglas J. *Ambition and Arrogance: Cardinal William O'Connell of Boston and the American Catholic Church.* San Diego, CA: Cobalt Productions, 2007.

Smith, Stacy L., and Charles Atkin. "Television Advertising and Children: Examining the Intended and Unintended Effects." In *The Faces of Televisual Media: Teaching, Violence, Selling to Children,* edited by Edward L. Palmer and Brian M. Young, 301–25. Mahwah, NJ: Lawrence Erlbaum Associates, 2003.

Sporschill, Georg. "The Church as an Advocate of Children." *Concilium,* no. 2 (1996): 89–98.

Stortz, Martha Ellen. "'Where or When Was Your Servant Innocent?' Augustine on Childhood." In *The Child in Christian Thought,* edited by Marcia J. Bunge, 78–102. Grand Rapids, MI: Eerdmans, 2001.

Stosur, David A., ed. *Unfailing Patience and Sound Teaching: Reflections on Episcopal Ministry in Honor of Rembert G. Weakland, OSB.* Collegeville, MN: Liturgical Press, 2003.

Strauss, Gerald. *Luther's House of Learning: Indoctrination of the Young in the German Reformation.* Baltimore and London: Johns Hopkins University Press, 1978.

Sturm, Douglas. "On the Suffering and Rights of Children: Toward a Theology of Childhood Liberation." *Cross Currents,* Summer 1992, 149–73.

Swift, Anthony. *Working Children Get Organized: An Introduction to Working Children's Organizations.* London: International Save the Children Alliance, 1999.

Theology Today 56, no. 4 (January 2000).

Thielman, Jeff, and Raymond A. Schroth. *Volunteer: With the Poor in Peru.* Bloomington, IN: 1st Books Library, 2000.

Tolfree, David. *Old Enough to Work, Old Enough to Have a Say: Different Approaches to Supporting Working Children.* Stockholm: Rädda Barnen, 1998.

Traina, Cristina. "For the Sins of the Parents: Roman Catholic Ethics and the Politics of Family." In *Prophetic Witness: Women's Strategies for Reform,* edited by Colleen Griffith. New York: Crossroad, 2009.

Tubbs, David L. *Freedom's Orphans: Contemporary Liberalism and the Fate of America's Children.* Princeton, NJ: Princeton University Press, 2007.

United Nations. *Convention on the Rights of the Child.* Adopted by the General Assembly of the United Nations on November 20, 1989. www2.ohchr.org/english/law/crc htm (accessed January 4, 2009).

United States Catholic Conference. *Moral Principles and Policy Priorities for Welfare Reform.* Washington, DC, 1995.

———. *Putting Children and Families First: A Challenge for Our Church, Nation and World.* Washington, DC, 1992.

United States Conference of Catholic Bishops. *Renewing Our Commitment to Catholic Elementary and Secondary Schools in the Third Millennium.* Washington, DC, 2005.

van Leeuwen, Mary Stewart, Annelies Knoppers, Margaret L. Koch, Douglas J. Schuurman, and Helen M. Sterk. *After Eden: Facing the Challenge of Gender Reconciliation.* Grand Rapids, MI: Eerdmans, 1993.

"Vatican Charter on the Rights of the Family." *Origins* 13, no. 27 (1983): 461–64.

Wadell, Paul J. *Happiness and the Christian Moral Life: An Introduction to Christian Ethics.* Lanham, MD: Rowman & Littlefield, 2008.

Wall, James M. "The New Middle Ground in the Family Debate: A Report on the 1994 Conference of the Religion, Culture, and Family Project." *Criterion,* Fall 1994, 24–31.

Wall, John. "Human Rights in Light of Children: A Christian Childist Perspective." Paper delivered at the Annual Meeting of the American Academy of Religion, 2006.

———. "Let the Little Children Come: Child Rearing as Challenge to Christian Ethics." *Horizons* 31, no. 1 (Spring 2004): 64–87.

Walsh, David. *Selling Out America's Children: How America Puts Profits before Values and What Parents Can Do.* Minneapolis: Fairview Press, 1994.

Weber, H. R. *Jesus and the Children.* Geneva: World Council of Churches, 1979.

White, Ben. "Defining the Intolerable: Child Work, Global Standards and Cultural Relativism." *Childhood* 6, no. 1 (1999): 133–44.

Whitmore, Todd David, with Tobias Winright. "Children: An Undeveloped Theme in Catholic Teaching." In *The Challenge of Global Stewardship: Roman Catholic Responses,* edited by Maura A. Ryan and Todd David Whitmore, 161–85. Notre Dame, IN: University of Notre Dame Press, 1997.

Witte, John, Jr., M. Christian Green, and Amy Wheeler, eds. *The Equal Regard Family and Its Friendly Critics: Don Browning and the Practical Theological Ethics of the Family.* Grand Rapids, MI: Eerdmans, 2007.

Williams, Rowan. *Lost Icons: Reflections on Cultural Bereavement.* Edinburgh: T&T Clark, 2000.

Wolfe, Alan. *Whose Keeper? Social Science and Moral Obligation.* Berkeley: University of California Press, 1989.

Wood, Diana. *The Church and Childhood.* Studies in Church History 31. Oxford: Blackwell, 1994.

Woodhead, Martin. "Combatting Child Labour: Listen to What the Children Say." *Childhood* 6, no. 1 (1999): 27–49.

Word and World: Theology for Christian Ministry 15, no. 1 (Winter 1995).

Young, Brian M. "Issues and Politics in Televisual Advertising and Children." In *The Faces of Televisual Media: Teaching, Violence, Selling to Children,* edited by Edward L. Palmer and Brian M. Young, 327–46. Mahwah, NJ: Lawrence Erlbaum Associates, 2003.

Zelizer, Viviana A. *Pricing the Priceless Child: The Changing Social Value of Children.* New York: Basic Books, 1985.

Index

About the Author

Mary M. Doyle Roche, Ph.D., is Edward Bennett Williams Fellow and assistant professor of religious studies at the College of the Holy Cross in Worcester, Massachusetts, where she teaches Christian ethics. She is coeditor of *Calling for Justice throughout the World: Catholic Women Theologians on the HIV/AIDS Pandemic* (2009) to which she contributed a chapter on children and HIV and AIDS. She lives with her husband and two children in Westborough, Massachusetts.